Essential Life C

Essential Life Coaching Skills provides a comprehensive guide to the complete range and depth of skills required to succeed as a life coach.

Angela Dunbar uses theoretical background alongside practical examples to provide a clear understanding of what makes a successful life coach. This book focuses on seven essential skill sets that are necessary for effective life coaching, with each chapter giving specific examples of how these skills are used in life coaching, and how they can be developed and improved. The book also includes a comprehensive, current overview of life coaching processes, practices and issues, from both the coach and client perspectives.

Essential Life Coaching Skills will be ideal reading for new and existing life coaches who wish to find ways to enhance their competence and ability. It will also be of use to therapists and counsellors looking to expand into coaching.

Angela Dunbar is a qualified life and performance coach, accredited with the Association for Coaching. As Managing Director of her own training and development consultancy since 1994, Angela coaches individuals on all aspects of their personal and professional lives.

Essential Coaching Skills and Knowledge
Series Editors: Gladeana McMahon,
Stephen Palmer & Averil Leimon

The **Essential Coaching Skills and Knowledge** series provides an accessible and lively introduction to key areas in the developing field of coaching. Each title in the series is written by leading coaches with extensive experience and has a strong practical emphasis, including illustrative vignettes, summary boxes, exercises and activities. Assuming no prior knowledge, these books will appeal to professionals in business, management, human resources, psychology, counselling and psychotherapy, as well as students and tutors of coaching and coaching psychology.

Titles in the series:

Essential Business Coaching
Averil Leimon, François Moscovici & Gladeana McMahon

Achieving Excellence in Your Coaching Practice: How to Run a Highly Successful Coaching Business
Gladeana McMahon, Stephen Palmer & Christine Wilding

A Guide to Coaching and Mental Health: The Recognition and Management of Psychological Issues
Andrew Buckley & Carole Buckley

Essential Life Coaching Skills
Angela Dunbar

101 Coaching Strategies
Edited by Gladeana McMahon & Anne Archer

Group and Team Coaching
Christine Thornton

Essential Life Coaching Skills

Angela Dunbar

Malule 1 : 1-29
Module2: 30 -54
Module3: 55 - 68
Module4: 69 - 98
Module5: 99 - 126
Malule 6: 127 -152
Module 7: 153-178
Malule 8: 178 - 191

Routledge
Taylor & Francis Group

LONDON AND NEW YORK

First published 2010
by Routledge
27 Church Lane, Hove, East Sussex BN3 2FA

Simultaneously published in the USA and Canada
by Routledge
711 Third Avenue, New York, NY 10017

Routledge is an imprint of the Taylor & Francis Group, an Informa business

Typeset in New Century Schoolbook by
RefineCatch Limited, Bungay, Suffolk

Paperback cover design by Lisa Dynan

This publication has been produced with paper manufactured to strict
environmental standards and with pulp derived from sustainable forests.

British Library Cataloguing in Publication Data
A catalogue record for this book is available from the British Library

Library of Congress Cataloging-in-Publication Data
Dunbar, Angela, 1964–
  Essential life coaching skills / Angela Dunbar.
    p. cm.
  Includes bibliographical references and index.
  ISBN 978–0–415–45896–2 (hardback) – ISBN 978–0–415–45897–9 (pbk.)
1. Personal coaching.   I. Title.
  BF637.P3D86 2009
  158′.3–dc22

                          2009007748

                          ISBN: 978–0–415–45896–2 (hbk)
                          ISBN: 978–0–415–45897–9 (pbk)

To Oliver and Jac, my two wonderful sons who with each passing day help me to grow up.

In honour of David Grove (died 8 January 2008) – a true genius whose ideas changed my world view beyond recognition.

Contents

List of figures

Foreword

by Carol Wilson

When asked to write this Foreword, I confess to having wondered whether the world needed another book about coaching; I was delighted and relieved to realise on reading it that the profession is moving far and fast enough to require the wealth of new information and insight that Angela has provided here.

Coaching is a wide and relatively undefined field, encompassing labels like life, business and performance coaching, plus a myriad of specialist types like finance or creative coaching. Angela's substantial experience in terms of both study and practical application are vital here, as she demonstrates that labels are of no great concern – what is being explored is a fundamental and specific process that produces extraordinary results, and which can be applied to any area of life or work.

One of the key principles of coaching is 'solution focus' – looking at what we want to achieve before we start. In true coaching fashion, Angela begins by setting an outcome as early as page 2. However, this is no ordinary goal because her readers are asked to create it for themselves, through a series of thought-provoking questions. Thus, a second tenet of coaching is honoured: 'self directed learning'.

Angela's book is cutting edge in terms of the peripheral issues she raises, including contracting documents, marketing and how to go about getting clients. Practical concerns are not forgotten, with sections devoted to supervision, accreditation, marketing and the differences between coaching and therapy. In my work at the Association for Coaching,

I find that these are the hot topics of the day and this book sets out a clear map of how the land currently lies, in a world where coaching has come to have a place in every large organisation across the globe as well as in people's day-to-day lives. All the content is backed up by a wealth of detailed case histories with explicit dialogue transcriptions.

What I liked the most is the extensive exploration of all the different theories and practices that are increasingly playing a part in the delivery of coaching, including Neuro linguistic programming (NLP), appreciate inquiry, transactional analysis, cognitive-behavioural therapy, counselling and David Grove's 'clean language'. Her exploration of the last of these, which has had little coverage elsewhere, is a treasure trove for coaches and I have to confess that I speak here with 'inside information', having worked with Angela for some years on Clean processes together with the late David Grove, who originated them.

There is a refreshing new take on areas that have been explored in other books, for example, discussing not just the building of rapport between coach and coachee, but also the dangers of having too much of it. After the framework and principles are laid down in the early chapters, we get onto the meaty stuff of intuition, with some fascinating information about the origins of the word, and some astute insights on challenge and motivation. Angela also guides her readers through a thorough examination of their own motives and values.

Whether the reader is a potential coach or client, or simply has a desire to understand more, this book provides an entertaining and easy-to-follow guide to what coaching is, what it does, how it works and where to go for the next stage of the journey.

Carol Wilson
March 2009

Introduction

Who is this book aimed at?

Life coaching is a new and exciting field of human development, with increasing popularity. If you are interested in
becoming a life coach, or have already embarked on such a
career, then this book will provide ways to help you understand and develop the skills required to excel in this area.

Life coaching spans a broader context than performance
or business coaching, and so if you work in a corporate
environment you may also find this book useful to enhance
your skills so as to widen the scope of your coaching and
treat your coachee as a whole person.

This book is also intended to be of benefit to therapists
who want to expand their current practice and become more
flexible when working with clients. By incorporating life
coaching skills, you can adapt your approach to become
more goal-focused and future-oriented. This may be provided
as an additional service for your clients or be included
within your existing service.

In fact, if you are involved in any kind of person-centred
occupation (e.g. doctor, teacher, nutritionist, personal fitness
trainer, etc.) the skills of life coaching could add to and
enhance your current service. By enabling you to understand
your customers more fully, you can help them to establish
relevant goals and find strategies to achieve them.

First and foremost, however, this book is aimed at *you*:
the very special and unique person who is reading this book
right now.

What will this book give you?

This book gives you a detailed blueprint of the key skills required of a life coach. You may be naturally very good at some of these skills, or perhaps have already undergone training in some of them. However, to be a well-rounded and successful coach, all the skills covered are essential. As well as defining the skills and breaking them down into specific areas of competency, the book gives specific examples and anecdotes on how these skills are used and how you can develop and enhance your own abilities in each area.

It should be noted that this book does not replace coach training, but it will support and complement any coach training programme that you undertake. If you are new to coaching, it will also help you decide on which specific skill-sets you need to work on developing further and how you might go about it.

Overall, this book will clarify your thinking about what is actually involved in the process of life coaching, and how the various skill-sets fit together to create a coach who can really make a difference to a person's thinking, beliefs, decisions, actions and ultimately their whole life.

Setting outcomes

If you don't know where you are going, you will probably end up somewhere else.

(Peter, 1977: 125)

This book is intended to prompt your thinking and stimulate ideas. This will enable you to take action and make decisions to improve your life coaching skills for your own personal benefit, as well as for the coachees who you work with. To maximize this impact, take a moment before you continue to read to decide on the outcomes that you would like to gain as a result of reading this book. It may help to consider the following questions:

- What do you want to get from reading this book?
- What specific answers are you looking for and what impact

could those answers have on your future career and life as a whole?

• What end result are you seeking to achieve by acquiring more information?

• After you have read this book, what would you like to have happen next?

Use your answers to the above questions to frame three separate goals in the space below. This will give you focus, with a clear end in mind and a reference point to refer back to later.

1

2

3

On a scale of 1 to 10, for each of your three goals, quantify where you are right now in relation to where you want to be. Are you starting the journey at a one or even a zero? Or are you already a few steps along, at three or four? Put your rating against each goal and, at the end of the book, we will come back to these goals to check on your progress.

How to get the most from this book

You may decide to read this whole book from beginning to end, to give yourself a good overview of the process of coaching and how it works. On the other hand, you may wish to dip straight in to the practical 'skills development' chapters, then work forwards or backwards depending on what grabs your attention. This is also appropriate and you may be referred to other connecting skills chapters at various points.

There are many practical exercises throughout the book that you can use to coach yourself. Alternatively, you could team up with a colleague and use the exercises as a model to coach each other.

It will be useful for you to regularly review your progress and decide on your next priority as far as skills development is concerned. You will find checklists and assessment processes throughout this book. These can be referred back to over a period of time to celebrate your progress and decide on further steps.

I wish you every success in your career as a life coach and I hope that this book will provide you with a springboard to your skills development that you will find both enjoyable and rewarding.

Life coaching in the UK – the story so far

What exactly is 'life' coaching?

Alicia looked and sounded nervous as she sat on the couch opposite me in my practice room. 'It's just . . . I don't really know where to start. I have been feeling discontented with my life for some time and it's hard to pinpoint why, or even when it first happened. Last week, I came to the conclusion that my job no longer motivates me, my relationship is stale and I have no idea what to do about it.'

'And is there anything else?' I gently prompted Alicia, sensing that there was more to be said.

'It's like; when I was younger I saw my life ahead as an exciting journey. I knew where I was going and how I thought I was going to get there. Now I've lost the map! And even if I had the map it wouldn't help me as I no longer know where I'm headed. So, is this the kind of thing a life coach like you can help me with?' she asked, looking me directly in the eyes for the first time.

'Well, let's see if we can help you find out more about what you want from life coaching, then you'll probably be able to answer that question for yourself. Would that be okay?'

Alicia agreed, and I began to ask her questions related to what she had told me, for instance:

- You mentioned your job and your relationship; what other areas of your life are important to you?
- And what's happening for you in each of those areas?
- When you were younger, what kind of exciting journey did you envisage?
- Did you ever experience that feeling of excitement? If so, how did you experience it? What was happening for you at that time?
- You said you don't know where you are headed. Where could you be heading?
- Where would you like to be heading?
- How could you find out more about where you want to be?
- If there were a map that could help, what kind of map would it need to be?
- What would you like instead of that job that no longer motivates you?
- Tell me more about your relationship that you say is stale. What needs to happen to change this?

By the end of our session, Alicia didn't yet have any answers, but she was beginning to understand the key questions about her life that she needed to answer. We were able to take those questions and turn them into three clear goals for life coaching:

1 To identify a job role that will motivate and excite me and create a plan to get such a job.
2 To build more relationships into my life through re-establishing old contacts and developing new friends.
3 To improve my self-esteem by losing a stone in weight.

So, Alicia had a clearer sense of direction, at least in the short term. And by moving towards these goals, the longer-term outcomes were likely to come into sharper focus. Over a series of six fortnightly sessions, I coached Alicia towards achieving each of these goals. I never told her what to do, I simply asked questions to

> help her explore her current situation and discover what needed to happen to shift her thinking. This in turn created positive behaviours and actions to gradually move her nearer to her goals.

The above story highlights the essence of life coaching as a method of helping a person to find out where they want to be, taking in all factors of their life, then working out a route plan that will help them to reach it. You can think of the role of a coach as a kind of vehicle – a method of transport to help a person get from A to B. The focus is always on moving forward towards an end-destination, the goal they have chosen to aim for, although a major part of a coach's work is often to help the client to define what that goal is in the first place.

So, coaching is about helping someone to achieve their own personal goals that they themselves set. The 'helping' can take many forms, always involving some kind of communication: either a face-to-face or telephone conversation, or, sometimes, in written form as an exercise.

In this book, the person who is being coached will be referred to as either the 'coachee' or in some cases the 'client', depending on the context. For example, when I refer to the process of coaching I use the term 'coachee', however when I am describing the business relationship that exists I use the term 'client'. Within the coaching industry, both terms are used to describe the life coaching customer.

Coaching involves asking questions to help the coachee realize previously un-thought of solutions. Most coaches do not attempt to provide the answers for the coachee – this would be more like the service provided by a consultancy. To continue my earlier metaphor: coaches provide the transport; they do not make the journey for the client. With coaching, the coachee must take responsibility for moving forwards; for example, by having the motivation to change and the commitment to carry out agreed actions.

Sir John Whitmore, one of the most well-known and

respected coaches in the UK today, offers this definition of coaching: 'Coaching is unlocking a person's potential to maximize their own performance. It is helping them to learn rather than teaching them' (Whitmore, 2002: 8). The International Coach Federation (2008) offers this more expansive definition:

> Coaching is partnering with clients in a thought-provoking and creative process that inspires them to maximize their personal and professional potential. Coaching is an ongoing relationship which focuses on clients taking action toward the realization of their visions, goals or desires. Coaching uses a process of inquiry and personal discovery to build the client's level of awareness and responsibility and provides the client with structure, support and feedback. The coaching process helps clients both define and achieve professional and personal goals faster and with more ease than would be possible otherwise.

While these definitions provide an overview of coaching in general, the following definitions from the Association for Coaching (2008a) provide a more detailed breakdown of different kinds of coaching:

Personal/life coaching

A collaborative solution-focused, results-oriented and systematic process in which the coach facilitates the enhancement of work performance, life experience, self-directed learning and personal growth of the coachee.

(Original quote: Grant, 2003: 254)

Executive coaching

As for personal coaching, but it is specifically focused at senior management level where there is an expectation for the coach to feel as comfortable exploring business related topics, as personal development topics with the client in order to improve their personal performance.

Corporate/business coaching

As for personal coaching, but the specific remit of a corporate coach is to focus on supporting an employee, either as an individual, as part of a team and/or organization to achieve improved business performance and operational effectiveness.

From these definitions we can see how other forms of coaching have the same common elements as life coaching.

Why is it called 'life' coaching?

'Life' coaching is the label that has been put on any kind of coaching that doesn't relate to business or sports performance. In life coaching any or all aspects of a person's life may be explored. So in reality, *all* coaching is life coaching because anyone being coached has a life that they can't just put to one side, whether at work or on the sports field.

If you decide to refer to yourself and advertise as a life coach, you will attract private clients who will have an expectation that you will be able to help them explore all aspects of their lives. This means that you are more likely to delve into personal issues and underlying beliefs, fears and desires than might be expected within a business environment. In this context it can be easy to get drawn into underlying problems that may be best dealt with by a trained psychotherapist or counsellor. To deal with this appropriately, a life coach needs to have thorough training and an appropriate level of skills to handle many different people and situations, as well as to know when and how to refer a coachee to a trained therapist.

In the UK at the moment, it is very easy to become a life coach, by simply calling yourself one, and promoting yourself as such. There has been a massive surge of new coaches over the last five years or so, but many are now struggling to make a full-time living out of it – and the competition to win clients is fierce.

To achieve some competitive differentiation, many coaches are specializing so that they have a specific niche, for instance as a 'parent' coach, or 'stress' coach. This provides a much clearer focus for business development and client acquisition, as you can clearly target and identify potential clients and adapt your marketing message to their likely issues and needs. In reality, a specialist 'niche' coach will still provide a complete life coaching service since, as I have already mentioned, specific life issues generally impact on and connect with a range of different life areas, such as finances, relationships, health, etc.

Life coaching versus business/executive coaching

Life coaching is a service that is paid for by an individual person, rather than an organization. In executive coaching, although the coach has a relationship with the coachee, the organization itself is the client since it is the organisation that pays for the coach. This can lead to conflicts of interest. Whose goal is the coach helping to realize – the company's or the individual coachee's? If a coach wants to remain in business, then satisfying their client's needs must remain a joint concern, if not overall priority.

Many executive coaches admit that, once a coaching assignment has been agreed, the work they do deals solely with the individual's goals. This could even involve the coachee wanting to leave the very organization that is paying for the coaching. Also, the coachee may well set goals and raise issues outside the scope of their work, including their health, home life, etc.

One key difference between executive and life coaching is the depth and breadth of what could be covered within a coaching session. An executive coach can be more directive in focusing on business/management issues and objectives. A life coach, on the other hand, is more likely to follow the client's direction, wherever it may go. However, the coaching skills employed and the coaching models and processes used are likely to be very similar, if not identical.

Another key difference between executive and life coaching seems to be what you can charge. Despite the similarity in skills and approach, in 2004 the average cost per hour coaching session for an executive coach was £125 to £250, while life coaching was £50 to £75 (Association for Coaching, 2004).

Where life coaching has come from

The Ancient Greeks put much energy and effort into helping their athletes achieve greater performance. These people were probably the first official coaches to ever exist, turning naturally gifted people with potential into Olympic champions.

In today's world, we associate the word 'coach' probably first and foremost with a sports coach. Almost all keen sportspeople – both amateur and professional – will employ a coach to help them improve their performance.

Outside of the sporting world, coaching has been understood and recognized as a management tool for performance improvement since at least the 1950s. But the story of life coaching as we know it today really began in the 1970s, when the Western world saw a 'new age' wave of interest in spirituality and self-improvement, and Timothy Gallwey, in his book *The Inner Game of Tennis* (Gallwey, 1974), popularized the link between physical performance and the power of the mind. By the 1980s, the first seeds of life coaching were sown in the UK by Sir John Whitmore, who adopted Gallwey's ideas and developed them into a process for people development.

Over the next decade, coaching became established as a profession, with an abundance of coaching schools and courses emerging throughout the world. By the beginning of the 21st century, many professional associations had been established to support the fledgling profession.

Since then, each new coach has influenced the profession by bringing to it their own ideas and perspectives, drawing from all manner of different backgrounds and education, theories and practice. All these different strands of thinking now knit together into the diverse and eclectic service known as life coaching.

Many of the models, theories and processes adopted within life coaching come from the field of psychology. Indeed, many counsellors and psychotherapists have branched into life coaching, bringing with them a wide range of approaches that have evolved over the last hundred years or so.

So, although life coaching is a new profession, its roots lie in established psychological theories and approaches: using concepts and ideas from traditional psychoanalysis and behaviourism, and people-centred strategies from humanistic and transpersonal psychology. Elements from all these aspects of psychology are likely to be covered in any good coach training course. In fact, some have become new 'branches' of coaching in their own right, such as cognitive-behavioural coaching and transpersonal coaching.

A further influence on the development of life coaching came out of the US in the form of neuro linguistic programming (NLP). Originating in the 1970s and founded by Richard Bandler and John Grinder (see, for example, Bandler and Grinder, 1976), this approach offered a 'user manual for the brain' with a set of processes and techniques to model excellence. Many life coaches study NLP as it provides useful frameworks and methods for helping clients to make behavioural changes and reframe negative beliefs and attitudes. Some specific NLP techniques and models that may be useful to a life coach are included later in this book.

In recent years, a new methodology has emerged in the form of 'clean language' and 'symbolic modelling'. The process of 'modelling' (from an NLP perspective this is about asking questions to learn more about *how* someone is thinking, rather than what they are thinking about) is used here to help initiate change without the 'ready-made' NLP quick-fix strategies. This leads to a non-directive, sustainable solution that comes from within the coachee. Again, there will be more detail about this in relation to life coaching further on in this book.

The growth of coaching

Since the profession began some 20 years ago, the growth in coaching in the UK has been phenomenal. It is impossible to say how many life coaches actually exist in the UK right now. Many people call themselves life coaches because they have added this term to a wide range of services that they offer. Others work part time in life coaching while earning their main income through executive coaching. What we do know is that there are a minimum of 30,000 coaches worldwide[1] and this figure is growing daily. The Association for Coaching is experiencing record numbers of new memberships each month and at the time of writing has over 2,000 members, most of whom are based in the UK. We have seen a rise in executive coaching with many large corporate organizations employing full-time coaches.

The popular online survey website Toluna conducted a poll[2] of nearly 30,000 worldwide participants. Just over 9 per cent said they were either a full- or part-time life coach. Although this is unlikely to reflect the general population, this high percentage does give some indication of the popularity of coaching.

Despite this growth, the average person in the UK still has little knowledge or experience of life coaching and how it could benefit them. Recently, I tried a little market research exercise and sat in the foyer of a local health and fitness club, asking everyone who walked in whether they had heard about life coaching and what they knew about it. Altogether I asked around 100 people. They were random visitors from a cross-section of people who were presumably somewhat interested in self-improvement by visiting a health and fitness club.

I was surprised to find that around 35 per cent didn't know what life coaching was. About 5 per cent thought it was something like personal fitness training. Another 35 per cent had heard of the term but, when I asked them what they thought a life coach actually did, I had offbeat suggestions like: 'Show me how to lead a perfect life' or 'Tell me how I can improve my life'. One person knew exactly what I was talking about since she had recently seen a life coach and had been delighted with the results. The remaining 24 per cent had a pretty good idea of what it was as they had experienced coaching within a work setting.

Many people in the UK have not experienced life coaching for themselves and so base their understanding of what it means on what they see and read in the media, where life coaching has become a popular topic. This can lead to misconceptions about the real essence of life coaching. Indeed, successful US coaches and authors Lynn Grodzki and Wendy Allen (2005: 13) suggest that media hype is presenting life coaching in a negative light:

> Life coaching has begun to be criticized based on its inclusion on a few TV shows. . . . In an attempt to make the process of life coaching more 'visual,' the TV coaches end up suggesting silly exercises for the women, which has left some in the viewing public scoffing at the idea of life coaching. Some in the coaching industry fear that the unusual portrayal of coaching in this show and others . . . will cheapen the perception of coaching, until it becomes the stuff of jokes.

For a new life coach in this emerging industry, the opportunities could be abundant as over the next few years the average person begins to recognize the benefits to be gained from personal one-on-one coaching. However, one of the fastest growth industries at the moment is coach training. This means that there are scores of brand-new, budding coaches just as keen as you to make their mark. And of course, not all will make it. The clued-in client will have a wealth of life coaches to choose from by simply picking up the *Yellow Pages*.

But how do these clients go about choosing a coach? The downside to this new industry is the lack of regulation and standardization of training and accreditation. This means that an unsuspecting client has no guarantee of coaching quality. Some life coaches have set up in business with no formal qualification or background in person-centred careers. Some have a pile of training certificates but may not have the requisite skills needed. Ultimately, clients will discover whether a coach is any good through their personal experience. In fact, the Association for Coaching now uses the term 'personal' coach rather than 'life' coach so as to differentiate the professional coach from those who may be jumping on the bandwagon of life coaching popularity with little training or experience.

As the market matures, life coaching clients are likely to look for guarantees of competence just as they would from any other service provider. The professional and competent life coach will gain business from word of mouth and their positive reputation. The poor coaches will undoubtedly have to find a new way to earn a living.

Getting adequate coach training is only part of the solution. Having a coach supervisor who regularly evaluates you and your client relationships is essential. But most importantly it's not the knowledge you have as a coach or even the techniques you use that will make you successful. It is the unique set of skills that you have acquired, through practice and experience (in coaching or a previous profession), that will make you a good coach.

Summary

- Coaching is about helping people get from where they are now, to where they want to be.
- All coaching could be defined as life coaching, although one way to differentiate personal from executive coaching is to ask: who pays the bill?
- Coaching is not new, but the *profession* of life coaching is, and the market is still emerging and likely to continue to grow.
- Life coaching is different from counselling or therapy, but many of the models and approaches from these disciplines are being used within life coaching.
- As the market matures, life coaches will need to demonstrate increasingly high levels of skill and back this up with suitable credentials.

2

Providing a life coaching service

Why people go to a life coach and what they expect

Anyone who decides to embark on the journey of life coaching will have their own unique reasons. However, it seems that the same kinds of life circumstances seem to trigger the need for coaching. All of us are likely to be affected by these kinds of circumstances, so you would be right in thinking that anyone could benefit from life coaching at some point in their lives. These life circumstances can be classified into five key areas:

1 *Something new has started* or is about to start
   For example:
   - new job;
   - new relationship;
   - new business;
   - new home;
   - new family circumstances;
   - new age decade, i.e. reaching your 40s, 50s, 60s etc.
2 *Something has ended* or is coming to an end
   For example:
   - a long-standing relationship;
   - family circumstances such as children leaving home;
   - a job;
   - working life, i.e. newly retired;
   - death of a partner or significant family member (usually after a delay of around a year – once the grieving process is over).

3 A *crossroads or dilemma* in their life has been reached that they need to resolve
For example:
- selling up and moving abroad or staying in this country;
- staying in current job or taking a new business opportunity;
- an either–or choice between two relationships.
4 *Nothing has changed and they are dissatisfied* with the status quo
For example:
- dissatisfied with job/career;
- dissatisfied with relationship;
- dissatisfied with their social life;
- recognizing that their own fears or anxiety are preventing them from making a change.
5 They have made *a decision to make a major change* in their lives
For example:
- get fitter;
- improve their self-image;
- improve their confidence.

Quite often, people will choose life coaching when a number of the above factors happen around the same time and they are overwhelmed and/or uncertain as to what to do next. Often, there are a number of different factors that clients want to address, hence the term 'life' coaching because all aspects of living can be dealt with.

How the client perceives the situation will impact on the kind of coaching that will suit them best, and its likely success. In the first three categories listed above, the changing circumstance is represented as an *external* happening that the client is dealing with. In categories 4 and 5, the change is something happening *within* the person. Generally, if the coachee 'owns' the change, they are more likely to commit to taking the actions required to make the change work. In contrast, when the client sees the change as something totally out of their control and something that they are a 'victim' of, they may find it harder to progress unless you help them to perceive their goal as something more self-directive.

Stages of change

A useful model to use when considering your client's attitude to change is Prochaska and DiClemente's (1983) 'stages of change model' developed in the late 1970s and early 1980s. In this model, there are six stages of change, and the coachee's perception of change and their attitude towards it will be different at each stage. How long each stage takes will vary tremendously from client to client since it is the individual who decides when they are ready to move to the next stage, not you as their coach. The underlying wisdom in this model is that the only effective and sustainable change is that which occurs as a result of the individual's decision to change, not by pressure from others. We will investigate this model in more depth in Chapter 11 ('Motivation skills').

Towards or away from?

Another factor to notice is whether the client is looking backwards (i.e. something ending) or forwards (something beginning). In the world of NLP, there is a model known as 'metaprogrammes', which is a way of classifying people according to certain thinking habits. One such thinking habit is this: people are classified as either *'towards'* or *'away from'* in terms of how they make change. The way they perceive their situation gives you an idea of which preference they have and can help you adapt your approach and even your terminology to better meet the client's perspective. For example, an *'away from'* person is more likely to be motivated to change by moving away from what they don't like rather than towards a goal they do want. With some it may shift once they start the coaching process, i.e. initially they just want to get away from the problem, but once they do that they can begin to focus on 'what next?'. More on this will follow in Chapter 11 ('Motivating skills').

The degree to which a client is willing to take ownership and responsibility of their situation will also affect how you coach them and their likely progress. 'Victims' may be caught in a pattern of behaviour and if you are not careful they will begin to blame you if they remain stuck.

Due to the infancy of the profession, your potential clients may not fully understand how life coaching is different from counselling or therapy. It is very important that you are clear about the service you can offer as a life coach and set clear boundaries. Learning how to deal with a client's therapeutic needs will be covered in Chapter 13 ('Understanding the difference between coaching and therapy').

Setting client expectations

Although life coaching is about achieving goals, many people will come to coaching with little or no idea of what their goals are. So, the first goal to work towards is often to define what it is they want from life.

Often, a first-time client has very vague expectations of coaching and it is vital that you help them to understand what is likely to happen during a coaching session. I have had some clients who expected that I would tell them exactly what they should do with their lives, and make decisions for them. You need to check what your client's expectations are and make it clear what coaching is – and isn't. Those clients who have previously been to counselling or psychotherapy may expect you to work in a similar way to what they have experienced from these professionals, while clients who have experienced coaching previously have a better understanding of what is likely to happen. In all instances, it is still worth clarifying their expectations.

Below is a simple document which I email or post to all clients before our first coaching session:

What is a coach?

A coach is a trained professional who uses various coaching methods, models and questions to help you achieve your goals.

A coach is different from a counsellor or a therapist, in that the focus is on moving forward, not necessarily to explore your past or uncover reasons for any problems in your life.

You may think that you can get the support you need from a good friend, however coaches do more than listen to you explain your problems, obstacles and wants. A coach will identify how you are currently thinking and behaving, and use this information to set you actions that will enable you to literally 'think outside the box' and move forward on areas of your life that you have previously struggled with.

Many coaches will specialise in a certain area, such as career, relationships or business. Some offer a more holistic 'life coach' service. Which approach is right for you depends on your particular reason for wanting to be coached.

Choosing the right coach for you

The coaching industry is in its infancy and there are many new coaches offering their services. Be sure that your coach has the right level of experience, as well as a professional qualification in coaching. Many coaches will have come from a related background, such as consultancy or counselling. As the profession of coaching becomes more established and professional, more and more coaches are becoming accredited and are investing in a form of supervision which acts as a 'quality check' to their work.

Questions to ask

- *How long have you been a coach for?*
- *How many paid clients have you worked with so far?*
- *Do you have a satisfied customer I could speak to as a reference? (Whether this is possible may depend on the nature of the coach's specialism.)*
- *Where did you train?*
- *How long was the training?*
- *What makes you different from other coaches?*
- *Are you or do you plan to become accredited?*
- *Do you have a supervisor or are you planning to do so?*

Going with your instinct

As well as looking at the logical factors, probably the most important thing is how you 'click' with the coach, so make sure you spend some time in general discussion to see how good the rapport is between you. The coach will probably start asking you questions, which will give you a sense of their style, i.e. hard hitting; caring; perceptive; enigmatic; direct; competent; professional; spiritual; creative, etc.

Taster session

Many coaches will offer an initial session for free or at a reduced rate. This will give you a further opportunity to decide whether this particular coach will be effective for you. At the end of that taster session, ask yourself:

- *What have I learnt from that session?*
- *Has anything changed for me now?*
- *What did the coach ask that made me think in a different way to how I have thought before?*
- *How comfortable do I feel with the coach?*
- *How clear am I on how this coach may help me to achieve my goals?*

Don't expect miracles in the first session. It takes a little while for the coach to get to know you and find what technique may suit you best.

Agreeing to work with a coach

Most professional coaches will ask you to sign an agreement, and probably ask for some money up front. You may be able to 'pay as you go', but to see the real value from coaching, you may need to commit to a set number of sessions over a period of time, i.e. one per fortnight for three months or one per month for a year. Be clear about what you have committed to and any cancellation clauses or money-back guarantees that apply.

Face-to-face or telephone?

Many coaches will work with a client by telephone as well as face-to-face. This is time-saving for you and the coach, as no travel time is required. Although the rapport may not be so strong without the face-to-face contact, many coaches say that this means issues and problems are addressed more head-on, and the anonymity means that honest, open communication is easier to achieve.

Most coaches will offer you a choice of face-to-face or telephone coaching. Choose what feels right to you and be prepared to experiment. A mix of both forms of communication, with perhaps some written exercises, would cover all bases and may be the most comprehensive and beneficial you could receive.

Being clear on what you want to achieve

The first aim of your coaching is likely to be to clearly define an outcome for your coaching sessions. Some people have a very clear idea of what they want. Perhaps they have struggled for many years failing to achieve that outcome, or maybe this is a new goal and they need help to work out new steps or strategies to achieve it. Others have a distinct sense of the problem or issue, but not much of an idea of what they want to have happen instead.

You can't move forward without having a focused, clearly defined goal to provide you with a direction for that movement. The clearer you are on what outcome(s) you want, the faster your coach can help move you forward (in general, but there will always be the exception to that!).

Take some time before your session with your coach to ask yourself the question: 'What would I like to have happen?' Apply this question to the coaching session itself, as well as your longer-term goals. Write down the answers to these questions and share them with your coach at the beginning of your session.

Taking action

Most coaching sessions will conclude with the coach gauging your commitment to carrying out certain actions. If there are any actions that you are not sure you can or will be able to do, say so at the time rather than wait until the next coaching session. The actions are for you, not to please your coach!

Write your actions down during or immediately after the session, and keep the paper or notebook where you wrote them down somewhere memorable, to prompt you to notice them and carry out the actions.

Keeping all your coaching actions, insights and thoughts in one notebook is a really good idea, as you can look back over the sessions and see what progress you are making.

Surprising outcomes

Sometimes people achieve exactly what they want to through coaching. Some work out what needs to happen for them to achieve their goals, and continue along their journey feeling revitalised and motivated.

Some may discover, through exploring their goal in new and insightful ways, that their goal isn't what they want after all. A totally new direction emerges and the old goal is no longer relevant. This type of change can lead to dramatic transformations in one's life.

For some people, the goal for coaching is simply to find out what they want, and the clarification of a goal becomes the purpose of coaching. If that insight and clarity is gained, this can also make a huge impact on someone's life.

Benefits from coaching

A good coach will never tell you what to do, or lead you in a certain direction. Coaches help you to access what is already there inside your own mind, but possibly shadowed or hidden by mental chatter and opinions of *others. A coach gives you the time and space to think for yourself, and focuses your attention on what really matters, through insightful questions and exercises. Working with a coach provides the impetus for taking action and making changes in your life.*

How will you know coaching has worked?

For most people, the answer is so resoundingly positive that the question becomes immaterial. They know they have changed for the better, they can feel it and see it, others notice and comment on it.

For others it is more subtle. For this reason it is really useful to gauge where you are in relation to your goal(s) at the beginning of the coaching process. This is your subjective measure, but your opinion is the one that counts here! By assessing yourself against those goals (on a scale of 1 to 10) at the beginning of your coaching relationship, and again at the end, you can see what improvements have been made. Some coaches may use 360 degree feedback forms for others around you to record the changes they notice. Your coach may also notice changes in you that you haven't been aware of consciously and he/she may share those with you. For some people, they find it easier to notice changes in others around them, which have come about as a result of their changed attitude and/or behaviour.

An ongoing cycle

Unlike going to a doctor, who is there to 'fix' you, then leave you alone until you are sick again, coaching is for healthy, happy people who want more of something in their lives. Wherever you are right now, you could benefit from coaching. When one coaching goal is achieved, a new one will emerge. Coaching could be an ongoing process of improvement for the rest of your life!

Benefits of coaching from the client's perspective

The Association for Coaching's (2004) UK Coaching Rates Survey asked what clients felt they were gaining from coaching, and below is a list of the most popular answers.

Confidential space to talk/place to think

In today's world we rarely get the time and space to just be ourselves and share our thoughts, knowing that there will be no judgement or consequence, so this is of utmost value to the coachee.

Sounding board

A coach can listen to ideas and feed back what they hear, with questions to help clarify the reality of what's being said, and ensure any plans are well thought through.

New/different perspectives

As already mentioned, the real value of a coach is to ask questions that create previously un-thought-of answers. A good coach helps you think outside the box of your normal habitual thinking patterns to see things in a new light.

Activities to support the coaching process

Many coaches will encourage the coachee to undertake certain actions or assignments that will help turn ideas into reality and ensure that a new way of thinking does result in a tangible behavioural change.

Session notes

Most coaches will take notes and provide copies of these for the coachee, enabling them to review their coaching session and reflect on their experience afterwards.

Advice

Most coaches will not give advice as such, but will enable a coachee to take their own advice through the questions they ask.

Quality service

As with any service, clients will judge the overall package and look for quality in the whole service: from how you answer the telephone and how quickly you respond to emails, to the cleanliness of your practice room.

Honesty/person to trust

Coachees value the unbiased response they get from their life coach, knowing that their coach can be totally truthful with them as there is no personal agenda.

Developmental support

Many coachees will have a good idea of what is required to move them forward in their life, and simply having a hand to hold and a guide to light the path ahead can be enough to generate movement.

Confidence to take action

A life coach can encourage the coachee and help them to build self-confidence by reducing any negative mental 'chatter' and creating the right state of mind.

Support a developing career

An unbiased life coach can help define career prospects and possible paths ahead, from a wider perspective than a line manager or human resources advisor.

Choices

This is the ultimate prize: greater choice means more freedom for the coachee to choose the life they want rather than the one they may feel they have simply 'ended up with'.

Most importantly, take time with each individual coachee to find out what they personally see as the benefit of working with a coach – and be sure to find out at the end of their coaching contract how that compares to what benefits they actually feel they gained. This information is not only useful to you as a coach, but will also be useful when writing your marketing messages as descriptions from real-life coachees will bring your advertising alive.

Importance of effective contracting

Having a contract between you and the client can ensure that clear expectations are set and both of you know the scope of the proposed coaching. It also confirms to the client that this is a professional and serious arrangement that requires a true commitment from them. In addition, it gives you and the client some legal protection in the unlikely event that at any point the relationship turns sour. As a minimum requirement your contract should cover:

- exactly what is being agreed to, i.e. number of sessions, duration of session, over what period of time;
- your costs and payment terms;
- what you provide within a session (it is impossible to list everything but a broad description of what you do and what the client can expect is useful);
- confidentiality – it is worth including that all information is treated in the strictest of confidence and none will be divulged to any other person;
- what you expect from the client (this could cover how you expect them to follow through on actions, when and how you expect them to keep you updated, etc.);
- scope – you may want to clarify here what is *not* part of the contract, i.e. matters outside of the scope of coaching that may require a therapeutical approach;

- the cancellation process;
- any penalty clauses that exist for cancellation or non-attendance of a session;
- any guarantees of satisfaction you offer (some coaches offer a 100 per cent money-back guarantee and I am sure this works to convince people to undertake coaching; however, you will have to honour this if the occasional unscrupulous person decides to call your bluff and ask for their money despite a job well done done).

Both the coach and the client should sign and date the contract, with a copy given to each party.

Although I do not have the space to cover this elsewhere in this book, the area of effective contracting is a critical one and could be seen as a coaching skill in its own right. To support this point, the Association for Coaching highlights the area of contracting as one of the 10 key areas of competency crucial for a professional coach (Association for Coaching, 2005). As a professional life coach, you need to ensure you have a contract that you have prepared thoroughly.

This chapter has served to set the scene for coaching by focusing on the client's perspective – why they may choose life coaching and what their overall expectations may be. This broad understanding may help you to focus more specifically on the actual services you provide and the unique benefits your coachees will gain.

Summary

- People will often come to life coaching because a major change in their lives has happened or is going to happen.
- As a coach, understanding the change process helps you determine where in the process your client is, and how best you can help them move forward from that place.
- How effective the life coaching is will depend, to a major degree, on how proactive and forward focused the individual is capable of being.
- As clients are often not well informed about what coach-

ing actually is and what can happen, it is vital that you set clear expectations at the start of the coaching relationship.

- Numerous benefits can be gained from coaching. The more you understand your specific target market, the more clearly you can articulate the specific benefits the client can expect to gain.
- To provide a professional service you need to have some kind of contract between yourself and the client, covering some simple but important terms.

3

Life coaching case studies

Life coaching means many different things to different people, and the process undertaken and results gained will be different and unique for each and every coachee. The following case studies present some examples of the scope and depth you may go to with your coachees and the variety of approaches that may prove useful.

Case study 1: Becoming the 'real me' and choosing the right path

This client first contacted me in the autumn, a few years ago. Our initial telephone conversation was a no-commitment, free 'taster' session. She very quickly began to describe her experience in metaphor: 'If I could just get inside my head, there is a piece of me that knows what would make me happy'. So, I started to use 'clean language' questions to build up her metaphoric understanding of what was going on. She quickly established a circular, bright orange ball in the middle of her head, and an ice pick that was needed to break through, but she didn't know where the ice pick was. This took all the time up in this first session, but the client made the decision to go ahead with a three-month coaching plan, consisting of one telephone session every two weeks.

The beginning – preparation and the first session

I sent the client confirmation of the structure of our coaching plan, a coaching agreement, a payment schedule and a detailed questionnaire. The questionnaire asks the client to clarify three goals to work on through the coaching plan, which I then use to provide an overall focus for the entire coaching. The client's goals were:

1 To feel more in control (that I have taken the postive action that I know is right for me), and be contented with myself.
2 To relate better to the people I meet and project an impression that reflects the 'real me', not the cross, negative, scary person I seem to have become.
3 To identify the job that is right for me, and go out and confidently interview for that new job.

Before our first full session together I reviewed all the information she had spoken and written about, and decided to use a variation of an NLP exercise: 'Who am I?'. The exercise consists of repeatedly asking the client to describe themselves, taking each description as a separate part and exploring the relationships between each part. The exercise was enlightening, and helped the client see the different facets that made up her complete self, and how some of them wanted different things. She had been spending all her energy satisfying everyone else's needs, but not her own.

After a session I always send a summary email to the client and ask for an email update before our next session. I asked the client to review the 'goals', and check that they were right for all the parts of her, and if so, to rate them out of 10. The goals were confirmed and ratings given. Although the scores were low, this felt like great progress, now we had clear goals to work towards and a numeric measure of where the client was. We had also established a good rapport.

The middle sessions

For the second session we explored the client's values around job satisfaction and employment, and that became the start of her quest for a new job. By the end of our first month together, this client had given herself a weekend away from home to write a seven-year plan on all aspects of her life – now she was very motivated and had a clear purpose!

The second month began with exploring the different options open to her in finding a new job/career. She described this as choosing the right 'path', from four possibilities she could imagine:

- Path 1: The same kind of role within a different organisation;
- Path 2: The same kind of role within the same industry;
- Path 3: A different kind of role within a different industry;
- Path 4: A different kind of role within the same or similar industry.

This led easily into some more clean language exploration of the 'path' metaphor, to discover more about each path.

The client took easily to the process, and I had the opportunity along the way to check in with the orange ball and the ice pick that was uncovered at the first session. The orange ball had been pierced in some way by the ice pick (now gone) and had turned into a beautiful flower with unfolding petals . . . it was a quite profound discovery for the client and seemed to change her self-image at a very deep level.

Around the middle of the coaching plan, the goals were checked, slightly amended and re-rated: Goal 1: 7/10, Goal 2: 4/10 and Goal 3: 4/10. She was making good progress.

More sessions revolved around exploring the paths in practical ways, such as researching job possibilities, clarifying the pros and cons attached to each path and the actions required for each. The basic strategy was that each path needed to be explored further before a decision could be made. Lots of 'What needs to happen?' questions drew out many actions, which were gradually progressed. Initially, Path 1 was the easiest: straight ahead and clear; while Path 2 was quickly eliminated as unattractive and unviable. Over time, the more mysterious and unknown Path 3 caught her attention, but ultimately Path 4 became the most compelling.

The final sessions

At the start of the third quarter, the client was actively applying for jobs and seeking/attending interviews. The paths were becoming clearer but still no firm decision had been made on which to pursue. The possibility of combining paths (i.e. part-time employment and studying for a self-employed career) was now becoming a real possibility. At one session we did a very practical 'SWOT' analysis, exploring the strengths and weaknesses that she could bring to a potential job role, compared to the opportunities and threats that a major career switch presented. From this, further clarification was gained.

We gave the goals a final review and she gave each a higher rating. Then, as a final exercise, I did an NLP 'time line' exercise with her. I asked her to imagine travelling along her time line to a point in the future when all these goals had been completely realised and to see herself sitting in front of her future self, listening to the advice her future self would offer. The key learning points that came up for her were around taking risks and moving forward. Finally, she travelled along her time line from the future to 'now', noticing all the significant events and choice points along the way. Something profound happened. We didn't talk much about it but I think she experienced a death or loss, which she realised she would need to deal with in the near future. Whether it was a real loss or some kind of metaphoric 'death' I do not know. It was a sad way to end the final session. However, the realisation that this would happen and that she would get through it would, I hope, provide her with strength.

Case study 2: Jumping off and becoming self-employed

Overall I worked with this next client for a total of 10 sessions, although I did not know that at the outset. This client did not make a firm commitment up front, deciding he would rather take each session as it came and decide then what would happen next. This was very much part of his make-up and was reflected in the way he tackled issues in coaching. Although overall there was a theme and a clear direction to the coaching, some individual sessions focused on separate issues, such as his relationship with his wife, which overall had a big impact on whether he could achieve his goals.

The initial session

This client was quite depressed at the start of our work together. In our first telephone conversation he admitted that he felt like jumping off a cliff.

Initially he set two goals for coaching – the first sounded like a higher aim for his life, the second, something more practical:

1 To make a difference.
2 To move from being employed to being self-employed.

In the initial session, he explained that he had tried a number of things that hadn't worked. He took clear responsibility for what happened in his life and felt that he had the right attitude and beliefs but was just not acting on them. He wasn't doing the things that he knew would take him forward. He admitted that he didn't feel happy very often and was disappointed by where he was in his life. He used metaphors about 'getting out' of where he was in order to make a change. I asked: 'where are you *now* if you need to get out?'. This led to a description of the prison-like stuckness he felt, like being in a cauldron. We then explored what would need to happen for him to be able to get out of that cauldron and the key resources that came up were: needing to have the confidence and courage to assess what was out there and make the right judgement.

With further questioning he realised that he'd lost his confidence a long time ago, when he was around 10 or 11 years old. In addition, he said: 'I want the confidence and courage to take risks, but if I take risks I am fearful of my wife's reaction, I don't want my wife's negative reaction so I don't take the risk . . . I have to not be me so she can be who she is'. This sounded like a mental 'bind' that was strong enough to keep him stuck in this status quo. We did some more visual-isation with clean language and found some useful sources of confidence and courage, although there seemed to be a flip side, in that in order to have the confidence and courage he required in order to make a living being self-employed, he would need to stop caring about other people. This seemed to go against one of his basic values (and overall aim – to make a difference) so no wonder that he didn't seem to be able to take the actions he knew he should.

By the end of the first session, we had identified many different strands or facets that could be explored as we moved forwards:

- gaining greater confidence and courage to become self-employed;
- exploring how the way he perceived his relationship with his wife was preventing him from taking actions – a convenient get-out – perhaps he wasn't so good at taking responsibility as I was hearing some 'victim' mentality regarding his relationship with his wife;
- misalignment between desired behaviour (confidence and courage) and values (to take care of others and make a difference).

The middle sessions

Over the next few sessions, we tackled each of these areas and more, swapping from sessions that focused on great self-awareness and understanding, to very practical 'strategy and action' based sessions. At the next session he decided he needed a much clearer goal for the future. At this point we were able to map out the goal regarding self-employment much more clearly, and then follow the GROW model (see Chapter 4) to highlight options and actions.

By our third session, the coaching was starting to have an impact on his thinking. He said: 'I'm a little more calm, less panicky and more patient. I've started to take myself more seriously'. We explored 'confidence and courage' in more detail, and examined the misalignment with his values. We explored the two 'parts' of him that wanted something different, using an NLP 'parts integration' exercise. By exploring the part that wants to care for others and make a difference, compared to the part that wants to be confident and courageous, some understanding of a different way to be self-employed began to emerge for him.

By the fourth session, something very significant shifted in that he took action and handed in his resignation at his employment. He said: 'I feel quite excited and free. My wife is being more supportive this time round'. However, the changes were also feeling a little uncomfortable and 'clunky': 'It feels like a bike, which is a bit wobbly, I need to tighten the nuts!' We spent the rest of this session going over the actions and the specific behaviours needed to support them. He set specific dates and agreed the evidence he would use to assess successful implementation.

At the fifth session we reviewed the past, present and future in terms of the coaching and how he was making progress towards his goal/overall aim in life. He described the *past* as being stuck, in something gloomy, and having low self-esteem. The *present* was appetising and fresh, and his state of mind was much more positive: 'I'm able to express myself more freely and I'm confident enough to find myself a way of living'. He described his relationship with his wife as more healthy, although he still felt he needed to be careful: it was like an egg – 'rather delicate'. The *future* was addressed with clearer goal setting and planning around the different areas of his life, which included current/immediate job situation, future self-employment business opportunities, goals around 'self' and goals around his 'relationship'. We used a business planning model to help him articulate where he was and where he wanted to be in all these areas. His assignment after the coaching session was to write up his own clearly detailed plan of action, which included specific calendar entries and even a daily time-management plan to ensure he spent the right amount of time working on all aspects of his life.

With the practical and the tangible very clearly defined and a way forward mapped out, in subsequent sessions we explored the higher values that subconsciously ruled his actions, then spent two whole sessions exploring his relationship with his wife, which I had felt from the start was a key issue for him and was impacting on all areas of his life. However, I waited until he raised it as the focus for the session.

Again, metaphors revealed much about how he perceived things and also the nature of the problem. He described a negative 'cycle' where the relationship went through periods of warmth, then became 'too hot', before turning icy cold. It could then take many weeks to warm up again. An unbreakable circle that he felt he had no control of. Initially he described his wife as controlling the cycle but after deeper examination and putting himself in his wife's shoes he was able to see this cycle as a self-generating system, where both he and his wife were inadvertently influencing this circular pattern of relating. By the end of the session he had a clear vision of how he would like it to be, the circle now a straight line – stretched out in front, leading to the future life that he had always wanted, living in the house of his dreams, in the place he most wanted to be, being self-employed so he has the time, energy and resources to pursue all his creative and altruistic interests and aims in life as well.

This is when his real vision for the future seemed to really come alive. And after the session he was able to articulate it to his wife, who was moved by it and very much wanted the same thing. The shift in their relationship dynamic was very noticeable: now he was being himself and she was able to go forwards with him, rather than her feeling stuck with him and needing to 'create a scene' to get some movement.

The penultimate session saw a rewriting of his overall life-plan that had been slowly emerging from our coaching sessions. Becoming self-employed was now part of a bigger process to become independent in many different ways. Now he was in a contract role, with much greater autonomy, but had not attained the ultimate dream of running his own business. This was, however, a considerable step nearer. The reality of potential failure in the high-risk business sector he wanted to work within had now sunk in and he had decided on a measured and careful strategy that would keep him and his family safe from bankruptcy, honouring his higher values.

Final session

A final review of all the areas of his life that had been covered during the coaching sessions revealed big improvements in 'self' – both in esteem and confidence. His work situation had changed totally, as he was now doing contract work, which had just been extended by a further three months. As far as his own business plans were concerned, the immediacy he felt in the first few sessions had abated. Now he was prepared to bide his time and get it right. Furthermore, his business plans were also now wrapped up in various other decisions such as whether to move house, whether to buy or rent, which schools to send the children to, etc. His relationship with his wife was still the greatest challenge. He could sense that the cycle could come back unless he got clearer about the future, and again verbalise this to his wife.

This felt like a good time for this client to continue on the path to independency by stopping our coaching sessions. We agreed that he could review this in six months and could continue with further sessions then, once the next steps in his plans had been realised.

Case study 3: Transcript of a clean language session

The following is a short telephone demonstration session, where I coached a fellow coach, Christine Compton[1]. We explored where her strengths and skills came from when she was coaching at her best:

Angela: When you're coaching at your best, that's like what?

Christine: It's magical and effortless.

Angela: It's magical and effortless. And when it's effortless, is there anything else about effortless?

Christine: I feel valuable. I feel ... gosh, 'vindicated' is the word that comes to mind. I feel my belief that when you are doing things perfectly it is effortless.

Angela: And when you are doing things perfectly, it's effortless. And you feel valuable. And when you feel valuable, what kind of valuable is that valuable?

---

[1] The transcript of this session is reproduced with kind permission from Christine Compton, www.christinecompton.com.

Christine: I feel my whole life has purpose. It has meaning. It's what I was made for.

Angela: And you feel your life has purpose and meaning. And when you feel valuable, whereabouts do you feel valuable?

Christine: I'm putting my hand on my heart, right in the middle there.

Angela: And you feel valuable right in the middle there, with your hand on your heart. And when you feel valuable, right in the middle, whereabouts right in the middle?

Christine: Right at the core of my being. Right at my very centre. Right at my heart.

Angela: It's right at the core of your being. And when it's right at that core of your being, is there anything else about that core?

Christine: I'm blossoming. I'm opening to my potential. I'm ... gosh, this isn't easy ... it's exactly I guess my whole life has meaning. It's what I was made for. It's my purpose. It's my reason for being.

Angela: It's your purpose. Your reason for being. And it's blossoming and opening to your potential. And when it's blossoming and opening to your potential, then what happens?

Christine: Then I just grow, I relax. I become who I am. I feel safe and confident.

Angela: You grow and relax and you feel safe and confident. And is there anything else about that confidence when you grow and relax?

Christine: I'm connected to something beyond. I'm connected to something bigger than me. Gosh, this is making me feel very emotional, I'm really surprised. I am connected to the whole. I'm part of the whole. I'm part of everything. I'm not alone. I'm not isolated.

Angela: And you're not isolated. And this is making you feel quite emotional. And you're connected to something beyond. And when you're connected to something beyond, is there anything else about that connection?

Christine: It's like it's everything that there is, it's everything I yearn for. It's everything I want.

Angela: It's everything you want. And it's a connection
to something beyond. And when it's a connection to something beyond, whereabouts is that
something beyond?

Christine: It's everywhere, it's everything. It's close to me
and it's way, way out there as well. It's . . . to me
it is the universe, it's everything that's a part of
the universe. . . . The whole.

Angela: It's the whole. And it's everywhere. And you're
not alone. And that's confidence. And that comes
when you grow and relax, blossoming and opening to your potential. And what happens just
before you blossom and open to your potential?

Christine: I feel a sense of opening. I feel real excitement.
I feel, again validated because it's what I've
always believed in my head but I'm feeling it.

Angela: You feel a sense of opening and a sense of
excitement and again validated. And when you
feel a sense of opening, whereabouts is that
sense of opening?

Christine: Again in my heart and the centre of my chest.

Angela: And what happens just before you feel that
sense of opening in your heart?

Christine: I can feel something like a starburst. A huge
firework going off.

Angela: You feel a sense of a huge firework going off.
And is there anything else about that firework?

Christine: It's one of those huge ones that bursts and
showers all those gorgeous sparkling lights.
There's something about it being very moment-
ary but everyone's witnessed it. It's like they've
seen it and they know it can happen. They know
that those fireworks are possible.

Angela: Everyone's witnessed it. And it's a huge firework that bursts and when there's a huge firework like that, where could that huge firework
have come from?

Christine: My logical mind keeps imagining people making

them, but it's something . . . it's the magical thing again. There's something absolutely magical about what can be created and the thrill that it can give. It's almost like it's . . . yes I know it's made by men but the end result is just pure magic.

Angela: Yes made by men but the end result is pure magic. And I'd love to explore this further with you, however would that be an OK place to bring this to a close?

Christine: It would be fine, and I'm absolutely bowled over . . . .

4

The life coaching process

Getting from A to B – a simple outline of the coaching process

In a nutshell, clients will come to you because they want to get to somewhere different from where they currently see themselves. That 'somewhere different' is their goal. It exists somewhere in their minds, and they may have a very clear idea of what it looks like or they may be somewhat hazy. What they *will* know is that they *don't have it now*.

So, if we take 'B' to represent that goal, then the client has to be at some point other than 'B', which we will call 'A'. The process of life coaching is to help a client get from where they are now (A) to where they want to be (B). There are many different models of coaching processes; however, they all relate somehow to this overall strategy of getting from A to B. So, how do you help someone get from A to B? The first two steps are likely to be about helping the client understand the difference between A and B by clearly defining their goal as an outcome and also getting a clear sense of the current reality (where they are now). What happens next depends on the client and the nature of their goal. It could simply be a case of helping them to explore options and coming up with the incremental steps needed for them to get from A to B. This would be a straightforward process of looking at possible solutions, strategies and actions and then deciding which to follow through. The popular GROW model follows this process and is widely used by life and executive coaches alike to help the coachee navigate a path to achievement.

The GROW model

Developed in the 1980s by a group that included Graham Alexander and Sir John Whitmore, this model for coaching has become the accepted norm for structuring a coaching session (Whitmore, 2002). There are four key stages to this model and, like building blocks, each provides the foundation for the next step. However, some flexibility is required as the coachee's understanding may shift during the session, at which point you may need to return to an earlier stage. The stages are explained below, along with other tools and processes that may be useful within each stage.

G stands for 'Goal'

This is the most important step and you are likely to spend the majority of your time clarifying the coachee's goals. As well spending considerable time at the outset of a coaching assignment agreeing overall goals, specific goals will also need to be set at the start of each individual coaching session. At this stage you will seek to clarify goals on at least three levels:

1 To establish an overall theme or topic that the coachee wants to focus on.
2 To work with the coachee to develop this into a clear, measurable and motivating goal to aim for.
3 To set the session goal in context with longer-term aims and objectives.

Generally, I encourage clients to set three overall aims or objectives at the outset of the coaching agreement, then review them regularly as the coachee makes changes.

Example questions at this first stage of the process include:

- What would you like to have happen?
- What area of your life would you like to focus on?
- What specifically do you want to achieve?
- If you were to achieve this, what would be different?
- What impact would achieving this have on other areas of your life?

Within the 'Goal' stage of the life coaching process, you may use other models or processes to help the client become clear on their outcomes, for instance the 'wheel of life' and/or 'well-formed outcomes'.

Wheel of life

The 'wheel' of life is a common life coaching tool used in practice, often to begin a series of sessions. It sets out a simple way of having the client think about all aspects of their life, not just the one key factor that has triggered them to approach a life coach. This could be a simple pre-session assignment that you ask the client to complete and bring with them to the first session, giving you the opportunity to explore the bigger picture in relation to the goals that they would like to achieve. The wheel consists of a circular diagram split by a number of spokes, usually eight, each representing a different major life area, such as career, finance, health, family, partner, social, spiritual and growth.

The client would then be asked to rate each area according to how content they are with it right now. They would mark the appropriate score out of 10 along each spoke, so that the more content they are, the nearer the edge they will be. By joining all the marks made on the spokes, you may end up with a wobbly wheel, highlighting the possible areas of dissatisfaction within the coachee's life. You could then use this diagram to help the coachee decide on which life areas they would like to concentrate on during coaching, setting goals for each.

Sometimes a coach may use a blank version of a wheel and have the client define their own aspects, which may be different to the generic list above. For instance, my personal wheel has just six areas, with 'creativity' being one and 'maintenance' being another. That is not to say that this is a better way to classify life aspects, just that different people may do so in different ways.

Well-formed outcomes

The following model has been developed from NLP and is a refreshing update to the well-known business goal-setting acronym of 'SMART' (Specific, Measureable, Aspirational and Agreed, Realistic/Relevant and Time-bound). You can use it as a questioning structure to ensure that your coachee has clearly defined goals and knows the overall impact they may have. With this understanding, the coachee is likely to feel more positive and motivated to take action towards achieving these goals.

Use the following questions as a checklist to explore your client's stated goals:

- Is the goal stated positively in terms of what the coachee wants to achieve? For example, a goal stated as 'I don't want to be unhappy' is not stated positively because the problem is contained in the language used and the client is likely to be focusing backwards and on the problem rather than the solution. Counter this with:
  - ◦ 'So, if you don't want to be unhappy, what do you want?'
- Can the coachee describe the goal in sensory-based language? Ask these questions to build a clearer multi-sensory understanding:
  - ◦ 'How will you know that you have achieved this?'
  - ◦ 'What will you be seeing/hearing/feeling when you have achieved this?'
- Is the goal self-initiated and self-controlled? Ask:
  - ◦ 'How can you control/influence this?'
- Ensure that the goal is appropriately contextualized. Ask:
  - ◦ 'When/where do you want this outcome? When/where don't you want this outcome?'
- Does the goal maintain appropriate 'secondary gain'? 'Secondary gain' refers to the subconscious positive 'payback' that the coachee may be getting from *not* achieving the goal. Ask:
  - ◦ 'What would you lose if you achieve this?' (Explore any loss that might not be welcomed. How can they keep the real or imagined payback? Or: what needs to happen for them to deal with this loss?)
- Ensure that the coachee builds in/includes the needed resources into the formulation of the goal. Ask:
  - ◦ 'What do you need to do to achieve this?'
  - ◦ 'Who can help you achieve this?'
- Ensure that the coachee attends to the ecology of the

whole 'system' (i.e. the goal has positive value for the coachee in a wider context, such as other areas of their life, their family, etc.)

o 'What else happens when you achieve this?'
o 'Who else might this affect?'

R stands for 'Reality Now'

At this stage you are finding out about the client's actual situation. You will explore whatever is in the client's perception as to where they are now. This is likely to include and uncover their beliefs, previous history, actual circumstances, perceived barriers and resources that may help them. You will also discover any actions or strategies the coachee has already tried in order to move towards their goal. Although a very important step in the life coaching process, it is easy to spend a whole session doing nothing but allowing the client to talk about themselves and their current reality. In itself, this is unlikely to move them forward. In fact, it could help to further cement their inertia by further reinforcing current habits of thinking.

Knowing how much information to gather at this stage is a valuable quality for a coach to have. This comes from having good listening, questioning and intuition skills, which are covered in Chapters 7, 8 and 9, respectively.

Carol Wilson, author of *Best Practice in Performance Coaching* (2007) and long-time business associate of Sir John Whitmore, has this to say about 'reality now' questions: 'you are inviting coachees to look at their current situation from different angles and perspectives, and it is this that will bring them new insight and awareness, which will in turn deliver clarity on how to move forward' (Wilson, 2007: 36). At this stage, you may use a psychometric test to help the client gain further insights into their current situation, particularly around understanding themselves and becoming more aware of any 'blind spots' they may have. Many psychometric tests require you to have specialist training to be able to interpret the results and give accurate, relevant and appropriate feedback. You may also use your own questionnaire for the client to complete, in writing, allowing them to share as much as they need to about their current situation. I find it useful to have the client complete this before the first session, or immediately after the first session.

Example questions at this stage of the process include:

- So, if that's where you want to be, where do you see yourself right now?
- What have you tried already to help you achieve this goal?
- What's stopping you from getting what you want?
- What strengths do you have that could be really useful to you to achieve this goal?
- When you think about all that you have explained to me about your situation, what's the most important aspect that relates to the goal you want to achieve?
- On a scale of one to ten, with ten being the rating you will give yourself when you have achieved your goal, where are you right now?

You may find the following model useful in this 'reality now' stage.

The SWOT analysis

This is a way of summarizing a client's key understanding about their current situation, taken from the world of marketing, where it is commonly used as a planning tool. SWOT is an acronym derived from the words:

- Strengths
- Weaknesses
- Opportunities
- Threats

The first two factors of the SWOT analysis – strengths and weaknesses – apply to the client themselves, i.e. internal factors that they can control and influence. The second two factors – opportunities and threats – apply to outside influences and their implications, e.g. those things about their circumstances, environment and people around them that are not in their direct control.

This model is very useful as a written exercise after the first session, to help the client summarize all that is relevant in their life right now and see it all on one piece of paper.

There is often value in asking questions around how factors in one section may impact on things in another section. Often, strategies for moving forward will emerge from this.

O stands for 'Options'

This third stage is where the coach encourages the client to explore possible ways forward. Here, what's important is to encourage a different kind of thinking in the client. By opening up possibilities, we can help the client to think more creatively and positively about strategies and behaviours that could get them more of what they want and less of what they don't want. At this stage, any blocks identified previously may be circumvented or overcome in some way.

Example questions at this stage of the process include:

- What could you do differently next time that might get another response?
- How do you think you could begin to solve this problem?
- What might be the action steps you need to take to achieve your goal?
- Can you think of any strategies you have used successfully in the past that might help you achieve this outcome?

Here you could use any manner of creative thinking exercises – from a simple brainstorming session to an 'emergent knowledge' exercise (examples will be given later in this book).

W stands for 'Will'

This stage of the coaching process is about helping a client to prioritize and commit to taking actions. It's about agreeing exactly what will happen and when, and setting a review date. There is a big difference between asking a client 'Can you take that action?' and 'Will you take that action?'. The first is a question about capability and possibility. 'Can you?' means 'Are you capable of?' in terms of skills, resources, abilities, beliefs, etc. It is a very important question to cover with a client because if they don't believe it is possible, then it certainly won't happen. However, this is not enough. The

'Will you?' question is seeking a commitment from the client. To answer this in the positive, the client must take a further step and consider the actual 'doing', not just the hypothetical possibility.

Example questions here include:

- What's the first thing you need to do to make this happen?
- Can you do that?
- And will you do it?
- When will you do it?
- On a scale of one to ten, how motivated do you feel about actually taking this action?
- What would need to happen for you to feel completely motivated to take that action?
- What could prevent you from taking that action?
- How could you deal with these potential obstacles if they come along?
- Now we've explored how you will deal with obstacles, how motivated do you feel about those actions now?
- Would you like to write that down in your diary right now?

Other models for coaching

Having come from a sales and marketing background, I use a number of models and frameworks that come from a business or marketing perspective.

A basic structure for business planning

This is similar to the GROW model:

- *Step 1: Where are you now?* (looking at your situation from an internal and external perspective and creating a summary SWOT analysis)
- *Step 2: Where do you want to be?* (specific and measureable, qualitative and quantitative)
- *Step 3: How could you get there?* (creative thinking, broad picture strategies, not detailed actions)
- *Step 4: How will you get there?* (choose specific strategies from those explored)
- *Step 5: What specific actions do you need to take and when*

will you carry them out? (tactics, diarizing activities, calendar of specifics)
- *Step 6: How will you know you are on track?* (setting key measures and milestones along the way, deciding how you will celebrate success, enlisting the support of others in monitoring your growth)

Symbolic modelling – a framework for change using 'clean language'

David Grove (a renowned New Zealand psychotherapist who sadly died in January 2008) originally created 'clean language' as a therapeutic communication process that enabled a client to stay within their own experience without being distracted or influenced by the therapist's own ideas or assumptions. He discovered that by asking simple questions that contained as few assumptions as possible, he enabled the client to more closely engage with their own experience. He also discovered that by asking these questions of any metaphoric content within a client's language, the client was able to start 'thinking about their thinking' and reach new levels of understanding. For more information on David Grove and articles and resources in relation to his work, go to the following websites: www.cleancoaching.com and www.cleanlanguage.co.uk.

NLP psychotherapists Penny Tompkins and James Lawley undertook a three-year research project to model Grove's approach. They developed their own process known as 'symbolic modelling', which combines clean language with a more process-driven methodology. Tompkins and Lawley have written a book on this subject entitled *Metaphors in Mind: Transformation through Symbolic Modelling* (2000).

Symbolic modelling uses clean language within the following basic model:

- Find out what the client wants, and spend considerable time facilitating them to develop their desired outcome. This can be done conceptually or metaphorically. The starter question is usually: 'And what would you like to have happen?'

- Explore the effects of the desired outcome happening, i.e. the bigger picture/wider implications and any follow-on consequences.
- Find out what needs to happen for them to achieve their desired outcome (necessary conditions).
- Check whether each necessary condition is possible, and if so, what needs to occur for it to happen.
- Acknowledge any problems, blocks or issues that occur along the way and converte them into desired outcomes, i.e. ask the client what they would like to have happen in light of the problems or blocks.
- Continue to use the process, repeating stages as necessary, with the aim of identifying the first or most significant (and often quite small) aspect that needs to change.
- Mostly a change will occur spontaneously. For instance, the coachee will realise a new insight or change a certain belief or value. When this happens the change needs to be 'matured' (i.e. you need to ask further questions to follow the change to its logical conclusion and explore any knock-on effects) and this is usually sufficient for the client to start implementing the change in their life.
- Occasionally, however, the process leads to the discovery of circular thinking or a binding pattern. At this point, you need to start asking questions about the structure of the bind, enabling the client to consider it at a different level, and possibly setting a higher-level goal – beginning the process again.

Emergent knowledge

David Grove first created clean language in the 1980s and he went on to develop further therapeutic and/or coaching processes that emerged from his earlier work. The first main area of development was 'clean space'. This takes the universal metaphor of conceptual space and makes it physical by asking the client (using clean language questions) to find various spaces around themselves that hold knowledge. The client physically moves to each new space discovered and gains insight from the new perspective. For example, the coach would ask the coachee to first write their goal (or draw ıt) on a piece of paper, then to place it somewhere around them in a space that feels right. They would then be asked to find other spaces around them that might know something about their goal. The coachee is encouraged to move around and stand in different places and positions, until some new information or understanding comes up for them. The act of moving and standing in different physical locations seems to 'unlock' hidden parts of the coachee's thinking so that different information can emerge.

The second, more recent area of development is 'emergent knowledge'. Grove used the simple model of 'getting from A to B' with which I began this chapter, to highlight the process of any coaching or therapeutic work; in that many people will come to a coach after they have already tried the straightforward and simple, logical, direct approach themselves and it hasn't worked. Something is stopping them from moving forward, however hard they try. For example, the client wants to 'settle down and get married'. They are currently in a relationship but can't commit. The first logical step is to move towards a greater commitment, but every time they try and do this, something backfires. They get 'cold feet'; their partner seems to become more argumentative, etc. It's like the world is against them achieving the goal they are sure they want. The 'something' that is stopping them is very likely to be an unconscious belief or value that is creating an internal conflict that they are unaware of. Whatever that something is, you can be sure that it exists somewhere between the points of A and B, i.e. something within the framework of how they view the whole reality of the situation.

Sometimes, the way to get from A to B is by not taking the direct route (let's call it 'C'). For instance, if this were a real journey, there may be road blocks, one-way systems and all manner of obstacles if one tries to take the direct 'as the crow flies' route between one's destination and current location. In the same way, coaching sometimes requires us to take some detours if we are to ultimately help a client reach their goals. By asking a client to physically map out the spaces where A and B currently are, they create a third space of 'C', which is everything in between A and B. By definition, this must include whatever's stopping them from reaching B.

Emergent knowledge uses a variety of processes designed to help a person discover new information, currently outside of their 'small world' knowledge of A, B and C. The language used is still clean, but even simpler in structure and form. Grove discovered that, for most people, there are six different steps or stages that need to be explored before a client reaches a new understanding of their situation. For this reason, the emergent knowledge processes involve the repetition of questions six times. The questions involved in this process are covered in more detail in Chapter 8 ('Questioning skills'). Grove took on board the new science of emergence and the theory of networks in formulating the process and question set, and I personally have seen it work scores of times to great effect. It is a very different way to coach and one that I recommend you explore fully.

Importance of having a framework/model of coaching to follow

As a life coach, you are responsible for 'shaping' the conversation and moving it towards a clear outcome with committed actions to getting there. On the other hand, too much focus on the 'process' of coaching will leave a client feeling forced to move forwards against their will. As a life coach it is important that you know of a variety of different tools, techniques and models so that you can be flexible. All clients are different and some will respond better to one model or process than another. I have given very simple overviews to some of the key processes and models. If this is your first exposure to them, I strongly advise that you gain further understanding before using them with a client.

In Chapter 2 I mentioned the 'stages of change model' and this is covered in depth in Chapter 11. By being aware of this model, you can 'pace' the client and move forwards only once you have the client ready for the next stage. As a coach this can be frustrating since sometimes it may be that you need to do nothing else but listen to a client's description of the problem, because until they are truly 'heard' they cannot take the necessary steps further forwards.

Non-directive versus directive processes

Most coaching experts agree that a non-directive approach is most effective in helping a client create sustainable change in their lives. There may be times, however, when a more directive approach is required. We will cover ways and means to do this in Chapter 10 ('Challenging skills'). When a coach is more directive and offers suggestions or gives advice, then they are in effect acting in the role of a 'mentor'. Here one needs to tread carefully since it is easy to go beyond the scope of coaching and create client resistance, or worse, dependency.

Summary

- Coaching is about helping people get from A (where they see themselves now) to B (where they want to be).
- The GROW model provides a useful framework for the process of coaching: establish the goal; explore the reality now; explore options; finally, have the will to take actions.
- Setting clear outcomes is a vital first step to coaching and could take up to half your available coaching time.
- Various other coaching models exist to help the coachee plot the path between A and B, which may not always be a direct route.
- Having a framework or model in your mind is really useful; however, don't force the coachee along a certain path. Let them lead the way. This may sometimes mean breaking away from a coaching framework and responding in the moment.

5

Skills within the wider context

The foundations to build on

Before we begin to study the skills required to be an out-
standing life coach, I'd like to emphasize that skills alone
won't make you a great coach. Skills are those competencies
that you are capable of, learned through experience and
training. These competencies are then reflected by the do-
able, measureable behaviour and activities that you display
on a regular basis. Underlying your skill set are two other
important factors. Imagine that all your qualities put
together form an iceberg. Your skills are the very top of that
iceberg, visible to others. But underneath the surface, the
underpinning qualities that support and nurture those skills
are your areas of knowledge and your attitudinal qualities.

- *What we do* is the end result of our training and experience, plus our habits of behaviour.
- *What we know* is the vast sum of information we have
  collected and stored in our brains that will impact on
  what we choose to do and how we do it.
- *Our attitude* is the emotional framework through which
  we perceive everything. What we want to do (or think
  we should do) is likely to impact on the end result even
  more than what we are capable of doing. Our attitudes
  are shaped by beliefs and values about ourselves, other
  people, coaching and everything else.

Underpinning knowledge

In the world of coaching it is often stated that to be a great coach you don't need to be an expert in a particular subject, as coaching skills alone are most important in helping a client find solutions and move forward. On the one hand, I agree that if a coach has a wealth of knowledge to draw on, it may be more tempting to offer advice or suggest solutions rather than take a coaching approach. However, that doesn't mean that the knowledge is a negative factor, simply that the coach must use their knowledge wisely when working with a client.

Anthony Grant (2006: 77) summarizes how knowledge can and does lead to understanding, while lack of knowledge may imply ignorance:

> For the coach to be able to ask the right questions, the coach must have a theory about the issue, and a theory about what kind of question will best help the coachee articulate a solution. . . . If the coach really had no expert knowledge (or skills) or no theory about how best to help the coachee, then it is hard to understand why the coachee would employ the coach in the first place.

Increased knowledge in following key areas will provide a competitive edge and also help you describe and demonstrate your credentials:

Coaching techniques and models

As well as being highly competent in the techniques and models that coaches specialize in, an overall understanding of a wider range of different theories, processes and models will help you keep your techniques in perspective and encourage continued learning. This will prevent you from becoming 'blinkered' by one or two favoured approaches, which may not be right for every person or situation.

The coaching market

Knowledge about the market within which you operate includes: the customers, the training suppliers, the professional bodies, regulation, best practice and, of course, your competitors – direct and indirect. This knowledge may not directly improve your skills, but will ensure that you stay focused on what customers want and expect and how you must deliver in order to stay in business and be competitive.

Your client

An obvious point perhaps, but a key area of knowledge to constantly increase, refine and update is your client. The more you know and understand your client, the better the quality of the questions you will ask. As well as knowledge of each individual client, you need to gather knowledge on your overall client base. What do you know about your 'typical' client? For instance: average age, kind of issue, male/female, where they live, what they do, etc. This information will be vital to help you successfully market your coaching practice.

Your own strengths and weaknesses

No coach is perfect, nor should they be. We are all human and our humanity is what makes us special. Rather than pretend to themselves that they have no faults, the excellent coach is aware of their own blind spots and compensates accordingly. They know what their habitual thinking patterns are and how these might bias their opinion or action with a client.

An excellent coach is likely to be someone who has undertaken much personal development work themselves, and knows first-hand what it feels like to work with a coach. As a practising coach, by reflecting on each coaching session and noticing what patterns are forming with regard to your coaching approach and perceptions of your client, you can separate out your own issues and beliefs from those of your client. This is a key area that a supervisor can help you with. A skilful supervisor will help you become more self-aware, so that you can navigate your way through client relationships with a heightened sense of awareness, and make adjustments for any blind spots or biases you may have.

Self-awareness is listed within the *AC Competency Framework©* (Association for Coaching, 2005) as one of the 10 key competency areas that are crucial for a coach. Altogether, 37 competencies are highlighted, each with positive and negative indicators.

Your self-awareness needs to shine light on the very reason you have chosen the profession of coaching. People often come into coaching because they have a deep-rooted desire to help a certain kind of person to achieve a certain kind of thing. Dig a little deeper and you may discover that this is a projection of your need to find your own solution to a problem or repeat a pattern of helping a father, mother or close family member. Make sure your motives are not too close to your own personal goals or it will be very difficult for you to remain unbiased.

Business processes

Many good coaches find the nuts and bolts of running a business a challenge. If you are an independent coach responsible for finding your own clients, you are likely to spend the vast majority of your time in the early years of trading working at developing your business, rather than your clients. This is a fact of life and one you will need to understand and accept if you are to be successful.

Business processes include the financial side of running a business: keeping accounts and maintaining accurate financial records. They also include setting some systems and procedures to aid you in running the business, such as automated email responses, standard agreement forms, etc. Finally, they include knowledge about the process of marketing: what needs to happen for you to win and keep clients? With that knowledge you can make decisions about how best to market yourself. If you don't have this knowledge, you need to take steps to acquire it.

Up to date and available

Today's knowledge is out of date tomorrow. Crucial to all knowledge is having systems in place to keep it up to date.

Another important point is the accessibility of information. It will be impossible to keep all the information you have in your mind, to be recalled whenever you need it. Perhaps most important is knowing where you have filed away that little golden nugget of precious information so that, when you need it, you can instantly and easily lay your hands on it.

Having the right attitude

The right kind of attitude is not one single state of mind. There are a number of different qualities that reflect how we perceive the world around us and the way we feel about that perception. These attitudes stem from our beliefs and values, and all will impact on our perception – our window to the world through which we see, hear and experience everything around us.

If you come from a psychology background, you will know that people actually invent most of what they call 'reality'. NLP theories highlight the filters we use to distort or change what we notice. Modern mind and brain specialists, such as Stephen Pinker (1997), also confirm that the brain is a collection of organs that, among other things, pull together the data from all that we collect through our five senses, then we 'fill in the gaps' from our own stored knowledge. 'Seeing is believing', the old saying goes, but actually the reverse is true. You'll notice what you already believe to be true. So, attitudes tend to have a very real impact on your behaviour, and thus the results you achieve.

What attitudes will help us to work most effectively with a client? Here are those that, in my opinion, are crucial to the successful coach:

Being open and non-judgemental

This is about having a level of tolerance and acceptance that it takes all sorts to make up the world. It would be easy to slip into a 'telling' style with clients; telling them what they should or shouldn't do, or justifying their behaviour by explaining 'why' they are doing it. None of these are the behaviours of an effective coach. This attitude is about not stereotyping people and their problems. Each client must be treated as someone totally unique, and special in their own right. This sense of value will transfer to the client, and help them to value themselves.

Self-belief in one's own ability to help others

A coach needs to sound confident and self-assured for a coachee to have confidence in them. If you doubt your own ability, this is going to leak through in your communication and behaviour towards the client, possibly leading to the client's doubt in you.

Willingness to empathize with another person's view

This empathy is a prerequisite to building a strong rapport and to have the coachee trust you. It would be easy for you to put yourself 'above' the coachee, particularly if you have 'expert' knowledge and background. However, empathy allows you to truly enter the client's world and relate to their problem and issues as if they were yours.

Results-oriented

With a strong focus on the client, and good empathy, much time could be spent listening to many descriptions of the past and the problem. You must be able to get to the nub of the matter reasonably quickly and direct the client's attention to possible solutions, not more descriptions of how the problem manifests itself.

Impartial and objective towards the client and their problem

This attitude helps to balance the people focus. A danger for many coaches, I believe, is that they can take on too much of a client's problem. A coach could enter into the client's world too effectively, and not be able to 'shake off' that client's attitude and feelings. Being impartial is like a good doctor who effectively helps patients, but doesn't let them take over their entire life and leave them stressed and exhausted.

Focused on others rather than self

Most of us at times see the world through the 'me too' filter. This is where you relate everything that has happened to another person to your own experience. In a way, this is part of the process of rapport-building – where we disclose similarities with another to help build a sense of kinship. However, the effective coach must be able to step outside of their own self-centred focus and attempt to see the world through their client's eyes.

Patience

Some may say that patience is a skill. Even so, it also takes an attitude of mind. The client will make progress at their pace, not yours. Although always striving to move forwards, you need to let go of your own need to 'get somewhere' and let the client take the time they need.

A genuine desire to help others

If this basic attitude isn't present, you will soon lose interest in being a coach. If you have this basic desire, then it's likely that the role will fulfil you like nothing before.

Understanding how our skills fit into a wider view of identity and behaviour

Figure 5.1 highlights a useful model to help us see that skills do not stand alone as impacting on our success. Skills in this model reside within the capabilities level, somewhere in the middle.

NLP expert Robert Dilts (1990) developed this model of understanding different levels of logic (or neurological levels as they are sometimes known) as natural hierarchies

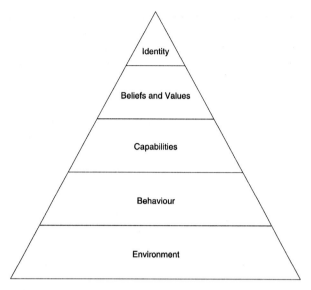

Figure 5.1 **Logical levels (adapted from Dilts, 1990)**

of classification, based on work carried out by anthropologist Gregory Bateson (2000). The key to success, according to Dilts (1990), is to ensure that all your levels are aligned. So, for a coach, this means that:

- At the top is your identity, who you really are and what your 'mission' is in life.
- Your identity supports the beliefs and values you hold to be true that impact on your coaching.
- In turn, those beliefs and values support you in developing the capabilities (skills and knowledge) you need to uphold those values and beliefs.
- The capabilities then enable you to behave in a certain way, which is aligned to all the levels above.
- The environment we choose to live/work within supports the behaviours we display.

In later versions of his model, Dilts added another inverted triangle above this one, which continued upwards with further levels representing the widening circle of influence outside and beyond ourselves as individuals, until we reach whatever global, all-encompassing wholeness that includes *everything* from our perspective. For some this may take on a religious meaning, for others a spiritual sense of inter-connectedness.

Dilts suggests that problems in achieving our goals are often due to some kind of misalignment or confusion at some level or other. For example, if we have a core value around 'it's not right to charge people for helping them' then our skills around marketing our life coaching business and the behaviours we need to use in our communications may not be effective in the long term. Somehow we will fail without knowing why. The higher levels override the lower ones, unless we can identify and address the core value that is sabotaging our success. The key to resolving issues is to work at the level above where the problem lies, as contained within each level will be the underlying beliefs and habitual thinking patterns that are likely to have created the problem in the first place. Dilts (1990: 209) explains this further: 'Changing something on a lower level could, but would not necessarily, affect the upper levels; but changing something in the upper levels would necessarily change things on the lower levels in order to support the higher level change'. As Einstein is often paraphrased as saying: No problem can be solved from the same level of consciousness that created it.

Clearly, this model can be a useful tool for considering your coachee's issues too.

An exercise using logical levels alignment

I suggest that to make this exercise more meaningful, you first 'map out' a giant triangle on an area of the floor. You can do this in your imagination, or you can actually create the triangle using bits of string, for example. This gives the added dimensions of space and movement to help us make the transition from one level to another. If you have a voice recorder then I suggest you use this to speak out loud the questions and then the answers while 'on your feet', rather than having to stop to write down any insights that occur to you during this process. Of course, you could always pair up with a fellow coach and run through this exercise with each other.

Start with a goal that reflects where you want to be with regard to life coaching/your life coaching business. Write this down as verbosely as you can, choosing each word carefully and adding any pictures or symbols that represent that goal to you. Now, you are going to explore the meaning of this goal to you through the different logical levels. Start at the widest point of the triangle, which represents the environment, then move along each of the other sections in turn, stopping to ask the following questions:

- *Environment:* Where do you need to be in order to achieve this goal? What environment will support you with this goal? Is there anything around you that may prevent you achieving this goal?
- *Behaviours:* What will you need to do in order to achieve this goal? What behaviours do you already display that support this goal? What current behaviours will you need to change?
- *Capabilities:* What skills do you have to support those behaviours? What skills do you need to develop to support those behaviours? What strategies, models and approaches do you currently use to guide your behaviours? What else do you need to learn? What do you know about your goal? What don't you know?
- *Beliefs and Values:* What's important to you about achieving this goal? What else is important to you? (Identify up to 10 values.) What's important to you about each of those? What do you believe about life coaching? And what else? (Up to 10 again.) What needs to be true for you to achieve this goal? And is it?
- *Identity:* Who are you when you achieve this goal? And who are you now? What's your mission in life? Does your goal fit with this mission?
- *Wider view/spirituality:* Step into the space that represents to you the wider community within which you live. Gradually expand your awareness to think about family, friends and colleagues; think about all the possible clients you might ever work with. Expand that view still

further until it includes all the people in the world. Then expand some more to include whatever else exists in your viewpoint, be that religious, spiritual or any other perspective. From this global perspective, how do you feel about your goal now? Does it still feel important and valuable? In what way?

Now step back through all the spaces you have already visited, and just notice if anything else occurs to you now at each logical level. Has anything changed?

To finish off this exercise, you may want to write down the significant factors that came up for you at each level. Only *you* will know if there is any misalignment. It may be obvious from what comes up, or may be more subtle, i.e. a slight feeling of discomfort at one level or another. If this is the case you might want to investigate this further with your own coach.

What it takes to be a successful life coach – key principles

As we have discussed already, in an increasingly competitive environment, coaches will be chosen and judged on not just their apparent ability but also the credentials that they can back this up with. To be a successful life coach means more than earning a reasonable full-time living from it. Success comes from a sense of satisfaction that you are doing the right thing and making a difference to people's lives. This, in itself, will impact on and influence your potential clients, generating a feeling of trust and confidence in you and your ability to help them.

It is important to take time to develop your own 'philosophy' on coaching, covering your ideas, beliefs and values around what coaching is and how you operate. The Association for Coaching's accreditation process requires you to put this in writing, and this can become a useful document for sharing with clients what makes you unique.

It is well worth presenting your philosophy in writing and being comfortable to talk about this to anyone who enquires. Below I have provided as an example my own coaching philosophy. I am not suggesting that it represents the 'right' philosophy, as we will all have different values and beliefs. It serves as an example of the kinds of aspects that might feature in your philosophy, formed by the experience and training you have received to date.

Example: My coaching philosophy

My beliefs and values around coaching are central to my overall values in life, and have formed over my lifetime of experiences to date, as well as specific coaching-related learnings.

I believe that everyone has within them all the answers that they need and they can discover for themselves the most appropriate decision. I wholeheartedly think and feel this to be true, and that each of us has the right to decide on our own path.

I believe that everyone has different thought processes, and is likely to think at a different speed to me. A coachee has much processing to do, and sometimes the silence between questions and answers is the space the coachee needs to come to their own conclusions. The change in a coachee often occurs when they have had the time to really think through a question or idea. I can best support a coachee by being comfortable with the silence, and allowing them all the time they need to reply.

The coachee's success is their success, not mine. The coachee is free to implement change, or not. My role is to encourage them to think of goals, actions and choices. I cannot make the change for them. I do not have to prove myself as a coach; I am coaching at my best when 'invisible'.

Every individual has the right to choose their own path. They alone can choose it, and I believe that each of us will choose the right path for our own personal development. I recognize that we all learn in life through our own choices, leading to a unique experience. I cannot choose the path for someone else. And I believe that whichever path they choose will ultimately lead to learning and development.

Personal integrity is one of my highest values in life; one must be true to oneself and have one's own thoughts, beliefs and values in congruence with each other. This influences my beliefs and behaviours as a coach, as well as influencing my ability to challenge a coachee who does not have integrity.

I value listening as the most important communication skill. To be truly listened to and so understood is a wonderful and rare gift to receive, and for coaching in itself will provide a safe context to make changes. I focus on the coachee's words, tone of voice, metaphors and beliefs and pace my questions accordingly, asking fewer, but more honed questions.

Values to abide by

If you join one of the main coaching professional bodies, you will be expected to agree and adhere to its stated values. In February 2008, the major UK coaching bodies worked together to create a statement of shared professional values (Association for Coaching, 2008c). The overarching aim of the statement is to continually enhance the competence and reputation of the coaching profession. It covers purpose, reputation, continuous competence enhancement, being client-centred, confidentiality and standards, law and diversity, boundary management and a personal pledge.

Summary

- Skills are the do-able competencies that can be observed and measured in your actions and behaviours. However, underlying those skills are your areas of knowledge and the underpinning attitudes by which you view the client.
- Self-awareness is a crucial dimension that enables us to know where and how we need to improve and develop.
- Skills can be seen as part of a greater model of 'logical levels' that make up who we are, what we think and the way we behave.
- To be a successful coach, all our logical levels need to be aligned to our goals.

- Your values as a coach will impact how you use any skills you have developed.
- Creating a written statement of your coaching philosophy is a useful way to gain clarification – for yourself as well as for your clients.

6

Relationship-building skills

The first skill-set that we will explore is that of relationship building. Unless you can effectively build relationships, you won't have clients to coach! And the kind of relationship you establish with your client will impact on the result of the coaching more than any specific model, process or skill that you can demonstrate. This chapter will explore how we build a relationship with a client, from creating a positive first impression to creating a strong and lasting rapport. But first, let's look at the wider picture.

Building client relationships – the wider picture

Let's start by thinking about how natural, social relationships are formed in the real world. Unknown people start off as untrusted strangers in our eyes, until we have an opportunity to connect and share information on some level. Usually, the journey to friendship happens gradually over a period of time as we become more interested in each other and open up more about ourselves.

Think of the courtship process that we all go through when forming a romantic relationship. There are some quite specific 'rules of engagement' that require a certain protocol to be followed, particularly in the early stages. There is something a little insincere and suspicious about a man who lavishes an expensive gift on a woman too soon in the court-ship. Or consider the woman who discusses favourite children's names on the second date. There are similar rules to follow when building relationships in connection with your life coaching business. By understanding these rules, you can employ the correct skills to help you at each stage of the relationship-forming process.

The 'funnel' concept (Figure 6.1)

The 'funnel' concept is an idea used by many marketing experts in many forms to explain the different steps involved

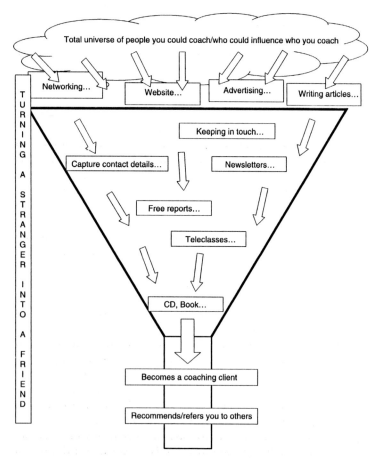

Figure 6.1 The funnel concept

in turning a stranger into a friend. Starting at the top of the funnel, imagine every possible person with whom you could coach, and every person who could influence others who may be coached by you. This is the total universe of your target market, and is likely to be a very large group of people, however focused you make your target niche market. From this 'pool' of contacts, some will be known to you, many will be strangers, many will cross your path now and again and gradually move into the funnel as a relationship is formed. A stranger may need to have a number of brief 'encounters' with you before they become aware of your existence. For instance, they may see an advert, read an article, stumble across your website, meet you at an event, etc. then next time they hear your name they say, 'I know that person from somewhere'.

At this point, that person has dropped down to the first level within the funnel: they are aware of you and remember who you are. This in itself means that a certain relationship has been created. They will hold you in greater esteem than a complete stranger (unless, of course, any of your actions have created a completely negative impression on them).

If at some point during these brief encounters you have been able to capture the person's contact details, you have an opportunity to keep in touch with them on a regular, consistent basis. As with a natural relationship forming, if any contact is seen as a bald attempt to have them buy from you, the bond could be broken. On the other hand, if you court your potential client by gradually giving them information that might be helpful and asking a little more about them, you have the makings of a trusting relationship. This is where a regular communication device, such as a newsletter, could come in useful, as you can give it to lots of people all at once and provide something of value for free. If you provide gradual information in this way, your potential client is likely to drop to the next level of the funnel, from 'I know this person' to 'I value this person' and 'I want to keep in touch, they have something interesting to say'.

At this stage, the person may be prepared to buy something from you. They are more likely to want to take just a small financial risk initially, like buying an audio CD or a book. They want to learn more about your ideas and want to do this in a safe way. Now your contact has become a client who says 'I like this person'. Over time, a deeper connection is formed as they move to the next stage of 'I trust this person'. Now you not only have a client (as and when they need your service), but also a recommender. This person is likely to talk about you to others and refer people to you when appropriate.

By understanding this funnel approach to relationship building you can make sure you develop processes and take actions that help everyone you meet drop through the funnel, gradually over time. Remember also to keep in touch with 'old' clients who have completed a series of coaching sessions with you, as these people will remain recommenders if you make an effort to keep the relationship strong.

Be seen in the right places

By 'right' places I mean the places where your potential clients go. Give yourself the opportunity of having brief encounters with people that can lead to relationships. Being seen regularly and frequently means that the strangers in your target market group will quickly begin to recognize and know you. The 'place' may be physical, e.g. your local gym, or it could be virtual, e.g. an online forum, or a magazine within which you write a regular feature.

The 'give' to 'get' mentality

By giving to people, unconditionally, without ever expecting to receive anything back, you create a positive tension in the dynamic of the relationship. Your generosity is likely to create a feeling of reciprocity in the other person. They will want to return the favour and help you out, by doing some good deed for you in exchange. Like the concept of 'karma', what goes around comes around and by getting out there and 'giving' of yourself, you will create positive connections with people with whom relationships will grow.

Within this you need to acknowledge your time and energy limitations and establish appropriate boundaries.

Participating in an online forum where you can offer suggestions and tips is one thing, providing a complete stranger with an afternoon of your time is another. What you give out needs to be in small doses and appropriate to the relationship, otherwise people may become suspicious of your motives.

Networking and the 'small world' theory of connections

How many people do you know? It is said we all have on average 250 known contacts. If each of those contacts knows a further 250 people, and each of those another 250 people, you can see how powerful the effect of networking can be, as expanding your contacts out to a friend of a friend of a friend means that your 'range' of connections and potential relationships has already grown to a massive 15,625,000 people! And that's only two connections away from your known contacts.

The 'small world' phenomenon is the theory that each of us is, in fact, just six connections away from anyone else on this planet. And by networking with our known contacts, we can have them help us to connect with the people who can help us achieve our goals, and connect us to those who need our help. This is a very powerful and organic way to develop your business through known contacts. Remember the 'give to get' principle to ensure that a connection with you is seen as valuable, and keep things small and appropriate/relevant.

Help others to connect

Think of relationship building as not just the points that exist between you and other single individuals. The power of networking lies in the interconnections and relationships that build right across your network on different levels and locations. This increases others' trust in you as a reputable person when you can put them in touch with someone else who can help them with something. You create a positive impression with two people then, both of whom will probably remember your introduction and reciprocate somehow.

Building a relationship with an individual client

The first few minutes of the first conversation with your potential client are extremely important. In those minutes your client will be forming a bond with you, based on their assumptions and beliefs about you as a coach and more generally as a person.

The term 'rapport' comes from the French word 'bring back' and a simple explanation of what it means is 'being on the same wavelength' as another person. When two people are in 'rapport', all communication seems to flow more smoothly, concepts and points of view are understood more easily and there is more likely to be a 'shared under-standing' and 'meeting of minds' as to what is being discussed. Although hard to define in a simple one-sentence explanation, we all know when we have a good or bad rapport with another person. It is something most of us can feel at a 'gut' level. We may not understand why we feel rapport (or not) but we recognise the feeling.

There is likely to be some level of rapport with everyone we communicate with, otherwise even the most basic form of communication would be ineffectual, as highlighted by Curly Martin (2001: 117): 'Rapport building is one of the most natural activities of human relationships and we are all gifted with the ability'.

As coaches we want clients to trust us and feel listened to and understood, so we must strive for an extremely high level of rapport. Once achieved, the client will open up and tell us 'the real story' rather than a superficial 'cover' to save face. The client can be themselves with us, relaxed that we will not judge or condemn them. Our role as a coach will therefore be much easier as the client will 'get' where we are coming from with our questions and will be following the same or similar line of thought themselves.

How is rapport created?

Rapport forms naturally with people who recognise a sense of 'kinship' with each other. The basic fact is that 'people like people like themselves'. With that commonality comes a sense of familiarity and comfortableness, which forms a bridge of openness and trust, allowing all communications to carry across easily.

Notice the natural similarities

The first step in developing greater rapport-building skills is to attune yourself to the natural similarities that exist between people that help form bonds. This could be their age, their background, where they grew up, a similar circumstance they find themselves in, shared experience, shared values, etc. The list is enormous and it is very hard to believe that it is possible to meet another human being that doesn't have a certain number of similarities with you. You can start to build great rapport by focusing on the similarities rather than the differences between yourself and the client. You don't even have to remark on them, the fact that you are aware and noticing for yourself will subtly affect the unconscious signals you are giving out and the client will find it easier to form a rapport with you.

You may occasionally choose to express some common ground you hold with the client, but beware of letting your own stuff out and messing with your clients! Keep it simple and brief. You may comment, 'Oh, I have a teenage daughter too, so I can understand what you mean by that', but don't be drawn into giving your opinion or telling your stories (unless you have consciously chosen to do this to help challenge the client's thinking).

Create similarities

Another way to increase rapport is to find ways to reflect back similarities that the client will see, hear or notice during your coaching session. This is a well-known NLP technique called 'mirroring and matching'. Mirroring is to 'copy' the coachee's body language, movements, voice tone and choice of words. Matching is a more general process of playing back something familiar, like tapping your finger when they are tapping their knee: not the mirror image but a sense of a similarity.

It is important to understand that people mirror and match each other naturally and subconsciously when they are in rapport. In creating similarities we seek to help a natural process develop rather than unnaturally playing copy-cat in an overly obvious manner that can destroy rather than build rapport.

Body language

It is useful to notice how a client is sitting and take on a similar pose. Cross your legs in the same way, tilt your head and/or lean forwards or back. You don't have to do this exactly or indeed all the time, just whenever you notice and particularly at the start of a relationship.

Becoming aware of a client's breathing and picking up on the same speed is a subtle but incredibly powerful way to mirror. This process can go hand in hand with deep and attentive listening. Smiles, nods and gestures are also easy to pick up and play back in a natural way.

Voice

A powerful way to build rapport is to notice how quickly or slowly a person speaks and use that pace yourself. To a lesser extent, the volume and the pitch can also be picked up and played back.

Words

Playing back the specific words a client uses has already been mentioned as a way to improve listening. It is also an excellent way of reflecting similarities, which can increase rapport.

Visual, auditory or kinaesthetic?

A basic NLP theory is that people relate to the external world around them through three key senses: what they see, what they hear and what they sense and feel. Each of us has a natural preference for one or two of these senses, and will use language that decodes our thinking. For example: a visual person will say 'I see what you mean'. An auditory person will say 'I like the sound of that'. And a kinaesthetic person (who senses and feels) will say 'I feel I can grasp that now'. Knowing your own natural preferences means that you can quickly be aware if your natural language is likely to match your clients and needs to be adjusted to speak the 'same language' as the client. For example, as a visual person I tend to use lots of visual metaphors in whatever form of communication I use. I'm a pretty strong kinaesthetic person so there will be a healthy dose of sensations and feelings to accompany my descriptions. I am, however, naturally weak on auditory communication. If I am working with a client who is a strong auditory person, I must listen carefully to reflect back the 'hearing and sound' based metaphors that the client will use.

Matching metaphors

Clients will almost always use metaphors to describe their experience of the world and what goes on 'inside their head'. Trust that this metaphoric description is truly meaningful for the client and that by reflecting back questions within the framework of those metaphors the client will feel honoured and understood, likely leading to a stronger rapport. For example, if a client says 'I'm stuck in this relationship. There's no way out', the metaphor here is one that a relationship is some kind of container that one can be inside or outside of. Develop a sense of curiosity about how someone structures their thinking when a relationship is like a container to them. How does one get in it? How exactly are they stuck? Do they ever get 'outside'? What kind of container is it? Is anyone else in there with them, for instance the other person in the relationship, or are they in fact outside, or even part of that container? So a question that reflects and honours the metaphor may be: 'And you are stuck in this relationship? What kind of relationship is one that can make you feel stuck like that?' or 'If there were a "way out" of this relationship, what would it look like (or sound like, or feel like . . .)?'.

More on metaphors and using clean language to explore them will be covered in Chapter 9.

Empathise with and validate their story

By acknowledging the client's experience and accepting their account, they feel accepted. This does not necessarily mean agreeing with them, just that you can see why they behaved in a certain way, or you can understand how a certain experience might have been difficult for them.

Sometimes you will have emotional clients who end up in tears as they explain something to you. If they have had a difficult time, is it helpful to show them that you are not surprised that they feel sad or upset and that it's perfectly natural that they would want to cry. This can be a release for the client who may have been bottling up their feelings for some time. Let them feel comfortable to let the tears flow, then give them a tissue and carry on coaching.

Different kinds of people need different approaches

This is a basic fact of life. Carl Jung (1992) identified different facets of personality that reflect a person's overall predisposition. Some of the most widely recognized are the terms 'introvert' and 'extrovert'. People are rarely either one or other extreme, but exist somewhere on a sliding scale between the two, and how closely you can adjust your behaviour to match their position will also improve rapport. Introversion will show itself through a need for more personal space, less direct eye contact and a slower pace. The introverted client is likely to pause for longer and give careful reflection before carefully forming words and sentences. They will also take longer to open up and talk about personal issues, preferring initially to explain the facts, talking about things and concepts. Also, they may be harder to 'read' as they may carefully hide whatever thoughts, feelings and emotions are running through them at any time.

Quite the reverse can be seen with the extrovert: they wear their heart on their sleeve and probably reveal all with a single look or gesture. They are likely to be up-front and give intimate details without any embarrassment. They tend to think quickly and talk even faster. They are more likely to get closer physically, feeling comfortable to lean forwards and look at you in the eye for longer periods of time.

Although these pointers are generalisms, they are definitely worth bearing in mind and will be particularly valuable when you are dealing with someone from the 'opposite' side to you. As such, it is important that you recognize where you are positioned on introversion/extroversion scale and make steps to adapt your natural speed, closeness and eye contact accordingly.

The building blocks to a good coach–client relationship

1 Create a positive first impression

Consider the ways in which potential clients will first discover you. It could be through an advert, your website, a chance meeting, a telephone enquiry. Also, they will discover you again in the first few minutes of your first coaching session. Take time to ensure that these various 'discovery points' really express the authentic you. By that I mean:

- Do you know what kind of coach you are? Can you explain it clearly in writing and in conversation?
- Do you have a clear coaching philosophy and can you easily describe it, and where it came from, to other people?
- Do you 'walk your talk'? That is, do you emulate the kinds of behaviours your clients are likely to want to develop in themselves such as:
  - forward focused;
  - curious;
  - open minded;
  - positive?

2 Unreservedly accept and respect the client for who they are

One of the most basic premises of NLP is to 'take on' a set of positive assumptions about yourself, the world and the people within it. These are known as 'NLP presuppositions' (Bodenhamer and Hall, 2002). These presuppositions are like 'personal mantras' that need to be believed and acted on 'as if' they were true. The following have the greatest significance for coaching:

- *The client is doing the very best they can, given their current resources* (resources include external factors such as money and time, but also internal factors such as skills, beliefs and confidence).
- *All of your client's behaviour has a positive intent* (however self-defeating or negative it may sound to you, from their perspective there is a 'good' reason for it).
- *The person with the greatest flexibility has the biggest influence over the outcome they can achieve* (with more options comes greater choice for taking different decisions, forming different beliefs, behaving differently, etc.).

Acceptance also means having empathy for who the client is and identifying with their circumstances, without pity or judgement. Remember that the client is a unique person with a unique goal. Don't allow your brain to fool you with stereotypical thinking such as 'This person is just like Mr X' or 'That reminds me of my own mother'. This person is a special, one-off, never to be repeated, version of a human being. Honour them for that if for nothing else!

Respect the client's superior knowledge of themselves and their situation. Bow to their inner wisdom and encourage them to connect with their own intuition. Respect their right to make changes in their life – and also their right to remain the same. You as a coach cannot force the client to take actions or break bad habits. Respecting that decisions come only from the client will not only improve your client relationship but also reduce your own stress levels! If you simply cannot respect and honour this particular client, then they are not the right client for you and you need to refer them on to someone else who can accept them.

3 Seek to understand before you expect to be understood

Take time to get to know the client. Allow them to express themselves freely without being in too much of a rush to get through your coaching model or NLP technique or questionnaire.

4 Accept that everything that the client tells you is true

It will be – for them. If you are hearing conflicting versions of the truth then you will need to challenge this (see Chapter 10). Looking for honesty and openness in your client means they are more likely to show these to you.

5 Take the first few minutes of every session putting the client at their ease

You can do this by:

- being relaxed and open yourself – be present, not detached;
- creating a sense of comfortableness between you by getting your tone of voice right and showing a relaxed demeanour with your body language;
- checking that they are physically comfortable;
- setting the scene by inviting them to share feedback;
- letting them choose where to sit, and where they would like you to sit.

6 Trust and have confidence in yourself

If you don't, your client won't.

7 Do what you say you will

To maintain a good rapport, the client needs to trust that you will follow through and do as you say.

8 *Act trustworthy*

As above, over time your client will form an opinion of how trustworthy you are. For instance, do you talk about other clients to them? Do you leave other clients' notes lying around? Do you belittle other people's views?

9 *Be available*

By this I mean that the client may sometimes want to speak to you outside of a coaching session. While it is important that you manage your time (and you need to set some expectation around this), providing the means for a client to make contact creates a sense of trust and continuity. You could, for instance, have 'open surgery' on a certain day between certain times, when your clients know you will be free and available to answer the telephone. Or you could advise them to contact you whenever they like, night or day, via email, whereupon you will respond within a certain time period. Or, you could just confirm that you will always read their emails and will review with them when you next meet. This is similar to the service I provide, and for most clients it is enough to know that they can reach me whenever they like; they don't need a response, just an opportunity to share their thoughts/experiences as they occur.

Telephone or face-to-face?

As you can see from the above, many aspects of rapport relate to what one can see face-to-face. So what impact does this have on telephone coaching sessions? Without doubt there is less to go on to consciously improve rapport. However, it can be done. For some clients, the fact that they can't see you means that they are able to share their thoughts and feelings at a very deep level, unhindered by your tangible presence. If this happens then their opening up creates a strong bond. Furthermore, without any visual 'distractions', you may find it easier to deeply listen to the client and in doing so improve the bond between you.

Over the telephone your voice skills become paramount.

Listen to how something is said, not just what is said, and match the intonation, pace, pitch, emphasis and modulation. By playing back not just the exact words, but in the same voice tone, you can create a sense of sameness from which rapport can emerge.

The danger of too great a rapport

Not all rapport is great rapport for a coach–client relationship. You are aiming to have a close but not too close relationship and sometimes that balance needs to be carefully maintained. Sometimes you may need to consciously reduce rapport because the client's attention is too greatly focused on you, rather than their goals, situation or strategies. You can do this gently and subtly by switching your attention slightly from the person to their 'stuff'. So, for example, look down at the paper they have written their goal on, look at wherever their gaze takes them when they 'go off' to think, look at their hands as they gesture, maintain good eye contact, but look at your notes a little more frequently. You want the client to be completely mesmerized by their own wisdom, not distracted by their attention of you.

Summary

- Build client relationships as you would natural relationships – turn strangers into friends over time.
- Remember the funnel concept and aim for brief, positive encounters, keeping in touch and giving to get.
- Use the 'small world' networking concept to create a wide network of contacts.
- Build rapport with individual clients by noticing and creating similarities.
- Adapt to different kinds of people by altering how you relate to them.
- Follow the building blocks to win trust.
- Be prepared to break rapport gently if it is distracting the client.

7

Listening skills

How often in our lives do we feel truly listened to and understood? This is a wonderful experience and a vital benefit that we provide for our coachees. It is such a necessary skill for coaching that we can easily assume we already have it covered. However, never take listening skills for granted because they are likely to continuously fluctuate and there will always be room for improvement.

Listening as part of communication

For communication to take place, we need at least two components: a sender and a receiver (see Figure 7.1). When it is completely effective, we would see that both the sender and the receiver have exactly the same understanding of the message. How often do you think this happens in reality? Probably never, or very seldom, as 'senders' can be unclear or incomplete in their explanation, and 'receivers' interpret the message using their own meanings. However, as coaches we can hone our listening skills to improve our understanding of the client's real message.

Imagine that communication is like sharing a jigsaw puzzle. When someone is explaining something to you, it is like they have a 100,000-piece jigsaw puzzle in their minds (after all, they know every single aspect of the message they want to convey). In a limited period of time, they need to transfer parts of that jigsaw puzzle to us so that we can begin to see what the picture is of. The effective communicator will select the appropriate pieces of the jigsaw puzzle to transfer

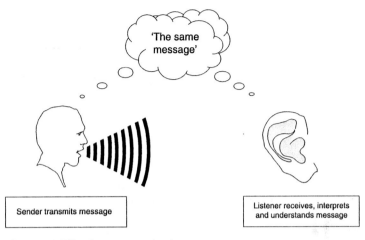

Figure 7.1 **Effective communication**

to the listener. The effective listener will look at each piece separately, but also compare it to what they have already, connecting the pieces to get a clearer sense of the overall puzzle. They will not 'guess' what the part is showing but use just what they see. Once they have enough pieces, they will start to 'fill in the gaps' of the picture. Maybe they have the four corners and most of the edges plus a few key items. 'Filling in the gaps' is what we all do, all the time, in order to reach an understanding of a message. A good listener holds back on filling in the gaps until they are sure they have the right picture. They also check their understanding to see if they have got it right.

Listening versus hearing

Most of us are fortunate enough to have good 'hearing', and we may hear whatever is audible to us, but active listening is something very different. As a trainer for many years, I ran workshops to help people develop their listening skills. I would begin the topic by telling the group that I was going to read out to them a list of 10 points – which represented the 10 worst listening habits that people are prone to. I'd clearly ask everyone to listen carefully. Having read out the list, I'd explain that, in fact, this was a test to see how well they were able to listen. I'd then read out the list again and ask them to score themselves a point for every one of the habits they had correctly recorded (they did not have to necessarily remember the points word for word, but understanding the 'gist' of each habit I described). On average, individuals would score five out of 10, which means that over half of what I said was being immediately lost, demonstrating that although we may well be hearing, our conscious mind has fallen into one bad listening habit or another! Some people would argue that this was a 'remembering' exercise. I would point out that if you have forgotten what the other person has said within two minutes of them saying it, then the impression it would give would be one of not listening! Also, I never prevented anyone taking notes (to support their memory) although people seldom bothered with this.

When people are just 'hearing' what's being said, in effect the message floats in one ear and out the other. To listen actively, the brain needs to get involved somehow. I have a metaphor of pieces of paper with messages written on them floating in through one ear. Then, as we consciously think about that information, it effectively 'staples' the information somewhere inside our minds. It becomes ours to keep.

In the training workshop I was able to prove this point. When I asked individuals to explore which of the worst listening habits they had recorded, almost without exception they said that they remembered those that they were most guilty of! This meant that they were more actively listening to those particular habits as they were processing the information – maybe seeing a picture of themselves doing it, or remembering a time, or thinking of an example. Whatever it was, they were participating in the process.

The 10 worst listening habits

Here are the 10 worst listening habits – if you want to test yourself, have someone read them out to you and see whether you can retain all the points covered:

- mentally criticizing the speaker's delivery instead of listening to their words;
- assuming that you already know what the speaker will say next;
- feeling such a strong reaction to what the speaker is saying that you stop listening and begin thinking of what you want to say in response;
- concentrating so much on the details that you miss the main idea;
- pretending to be attentive while actually thinking of something else;
- trying to take notes on everything that is said;
- remaining silent when you do not understand the message;
- believing that talking is active and listening is passive – and wanting to show how active you are;
- disagreeing with what the speaker says so you stop listening;
- letting your mind wander.

Is listening a skill or an attitude?

If we think of listening as something we do, that we can learn to improve, then we can quite rightly classify it as a skill. On the other hand, listening is as much about the avoidance of doing other stuff (those bad habits) and keeping ourselves receptive and free of distractions.

The first step towards improving your listening is to have the right attitude. Really wanting to listen and being in the right frame of mind to listen is likely to vastly improve your listening skills right away.

As a new coach, your enthusiasm and interest for the client is likely to help you to stay motivated to listen. After a while, you may discover that you are in danger of 'switching off' during a coaching session, just like in any other situation in your life, particularly if the subject is one that you have heard before many times, or the client's delivery of their message makes it dull and uninteresting. You may also find your listening levels affected by tiredness or hunger. Catch yourself drifting away and remind yourself why you want to listen.

Levels of listening

In the book *Co-Active Coaching* (Whitworth *et al.*, 2007), the authors describe the different levels of listening that we could be operating from. By understanding this model, we can recognize that very few of us will operate at the highest level at all times. We will 'slip' to the lower level when we are tired, stressed, or not placing enough importance on the other person's message.

Level 1 listening

At this level, our focus of attention is on ourselves. We may appear to be listening to others, but we are making sense of what we hear by applying it to our own thinking and frameworks. We have our own jigsaw puzzle and will match only the pieces that fit what we have already. With this kind of listening, misunderstandings are commonplace. We hear what we think the other person has said, as our filters on the external world will be set for 'selective attention'. We may become skilled at appearing to listen at this level, but the truth is we are motivated by our own thoughts, ideas and contribution, listening only enough to be able to follow the thread and score points through our own contribution.

This kind of listening is commonplace during an argument or a disagreement, especially if emotions are running high. We could also slip into this kind of listening when we are busy thinking of something 'more important', for instance our next coaching question. So we give lots of appropriate listening noises and say 'Yes, go on, I'm listening', but really our brains are engaged elsewhere. The other person will almost certainly know they are not being listened to.

Level 2 listening

At this level of listening, we are focusing very directly on the other person, and working hard to understand and assimilate the information we are hearing. We put together the words and data and interpret the information. We check our understanding and seek clarification when we are not sure. There is much processing going on here as the listener is gathering information, analyzing its meaning and forming a conclusion all at the same time. We are aware of the voice and body language and will use these subtle signals to influence our overall understanding of the message. This is an acceptable level of listening to aim for and one any good coach will be operating from most of the time.

Level 3 listening

At this level, our awareness has expanded to include ourselves, the client and everything around the client as well. This level of listening can be compared to how peripheral vision works with our eyesight. Instead of being focused on a single spot, our eyes are more relaxed and tuned in to notice what's going on in the bigger picture. At this level of listening, we are taking in a wider range of information, analyzing and interpreting less but allowing our understanding to emerge gradually. Now we are likely to be in deep rapport with the other person (or their story) and also able to access our intuition as we are 'letting in' as much information as possible, without judgement or criticism. Although not easy to achieve, once you are in this state of listening, it is actually easier than level 2 as it is less tiring, and a lot more interesting and rewarding.

Strategies to improve your listening skills

Plan to pay attention

Immediately before working with a client, go through the process of emptying your mind completely of any private thoughts or stresses that may take up your attention. This is more than just *telling* yourself to stop. It is worth developing your own kind of 'ritual' to visualize your own thoughts and emotions somehow leaving your mind and entering into some nice, safe place where they can be looked after until after the client session. When your own thoughts have been safely stored away, you can devote some time to re-reading any previous notes on the client to fully engage your mind with the person so that you are ready and 'in touch' with them from the very start of the session.

Exercise: Visualization to empty your mind before a client session

When you think about your own thoughts, whereabouts in your head do you imagine those thoughts are? Get a sense of a place, and then check where specifically *inside* that place you imagine your thoughts to be. Then imagine a place outside of yourself where you would be comfortable for them to stay for a short while. Get a clear sense of what this place, container or whatever looks like, then imagine it being in a particular space somewhere around, beneath or behind you. Then play with your imagination. Imagine how those thoughts could get from that place in your head to that comfortable place outside you.

With practice you can create your own effective visualization process for emptying your mind of distracting thoughts. Furthermore, I always find that, as a bonus, when I let these thoughts return after a short break, they always seem brighter and better for their holiday!

Staying out of the client's way

This means making sure you keep your *own* agenda/experience out of your perception of the coachee and their situation. The visualization exercise should go some way to help you to achieve this, but you also need to stay aware that your own thoughts, opinions, assumptions, beliefs and life experiences cannot help but shape your understanding of what the client is telling you.

If you have caught yourself jumping on a train of thought in response to a client telling you something of their personal experience, have you leapt onto the same bandwagon and are now recollecting your own similar experience? This is perfectly natural and almost impossible not to do. The secret is to come back from your own experience, hold that information but let go of that as the only possible experience and continue to pay attention and explore it from an 'unknown' perspective.

Monitor 'Self-talk'

Being aware of your own silent monologue as it chatters in the background is a very helpful strategy to improve listening. Work at turning down the volume or even turning it off, if all it offers are assumptions, judgements and opinions. Intuition tends to come from a deeper source and pops into your head as a complete idea, feeling or thought, rather than a stream of words.

Kinds of self-talk to be most aware of and learn to switch off are:

- *self-doubt*: 'Was that the right question to ask?'
- *impatience*: 'Hurry up, you only have 10 minutes left.'
- *fear*: 'What if the client doesn't like me?'

Show the client that you are listening

Typically, using plenty of eye contact, nodding to show understanding and leaning forward indicate that you are listening. If you are taking notes, ensure that your gaze is not too firmly fixed on your papers, rather than the client themselves.

Over the telephone, the client cannot see your reactions, so you need to allow them to hear your understanding through appropriate and well-timed 'mmms', 'er. .hums' and especially 'ah. .has'.

Use note-taking/recordings effectively

Personally, I find note-taking essential, although I know other excellent coaches who manage very well without this. As a visual person, it helps me to 'see' the client's words as well as hear them. If you are strongly auditory you may manage without them. However, some kind of record that you can refer back to at a later date is always very useful, so if you don't feel you need to make notes, you might want to consider recording the session. These recordings can also be immensely valuable to the client too, as it enables them to listen to themselves – something they may have never done before.

If/when you take notes, consider the purpose of those notes:

- *to improve your listening/understanding.* For this to work, you need only take a note of the odd word or phrase that seems to hold some energy. (Whatever you do, don't try and write down complete sentences or everything that the person says – you will quickly lose the thread of the message and gain no understanding at all.) You may also jot down a word that comes to you from your intuition. I sometimes even doodle a shape or pattern – which often contains some extra wisdom.
- *to use as a record to refer back to later.* In addition to the above, there may be words, phrases, names or numbers that would be important to remember and quote back to the client accurately in the future. Make a note of these too.

Bear in mind that any notes or records you keep about a client will need to be stored in accordance with the Data Protection Act.

Check your understanding

Some questions that you ask are to help you clarify your understanding of the client's message. If you miss the odd word, it can distort your understanding of the whole thing. So, be prepared to ask the client to repeat something, or explain further, or give an example, etc. so as to ensure that you have correctly gained the meaning that the client intends to impart.

Listen for what is not said as well as what is

This is a powerful skill to pay attention to and develop. There is an inherent logic to all statements that the client makes, and often there are clues as to the nature of a problem in the way that the client 'misses out' an expected element of the jigsaw puzzle. For example, the client might say 'This always happens to me. This happens every day. It happened yesterday, and the day before that. And it happened last week'. You may spot the gap and ask: 'What happened three days ago?'.

In NLP, words and language are said to highlight the thinking processes the client is using and, by noticing the 'deletions', 'generalisms' and/or 'distortions' a client is making, you can understand more about the person, their beliefs and values and what might be blocking their progress (Bodenhamer and Hall, 2002: 135–174).

Below is a series of examples of common deletions, generalisms and distortions, along with some suggested ways of exploring these further, whether as questions to ask of the client, or as overall strategies of investigating them during the session/ongoing sessions.

Deletions
Unspecified nouns: 'It just isn't working.' or 'They never listen.'

- What is 'it'?
- What isn't working?
- Exactly who never listens?

Unspecified verbs: 'She helped me.'

- Exactly how did she help you?

Missing comparisons: 'I feel better now.'

- Better than what?
- What or who are you comparing this to?

Generalisms
As well as actual 'gaps', you can listen out for 'generalisms', which wrap up too much unspoken detail in a single statement.

Universal quantifiers: 'It always goes wrong.'

- What, absolutely always?
- Can you think of just one time that it didn't?

Un-owned judgements: 'It's wrong to swear.'

- In whose opinion is it wrong?

Beliefs around what can/can't or should/shouldn't happen: 'I mustn't let that happen.' or 'I can't do that.'

- Why not?
- What prevents you?
- What would happen if you did?

Distortions

Finally, clients distort the information they give you in such a way that gaps of understanding are created.

Turning a verb into a thing: 'This relationship isn't working.' The verb 'to relate' has been turned into something that sounds like an object – a relationship – but it isn't really a solid thing you can see and touch. It is far more constructive to turn it back into the verb and explore further.

- Exactly how are you relating to each other that isn't working?

Mind reading: 'I knew she hated me from day one.'

- How did you know?
- What evidence supports that knowledge?

A vague 'cause' to an effect: 'He made me cry.'

- How exactly did he do that?

One piece of information is assumed to equal another, different piece of information: 'He doesn't care because he forgot my birthday.'

- Does forgetting someone's birthday always mean they don't care?
- In what way does forgetting a birthday equate to how much a person cares?

Presuppositions: 'Because she has a degree I knew she'd act superior and make me feel stupid.' There are many gaps in this one. The presupposing part is assuming that people who have a degree will act superior:

- How do you know that people with degrees act like that?
- What led you to that conclusion about people with degrees?

Listen for the metaphors/patterns

As well as describing thought patterns with words and language, there is a deeper structure of thinking that can 'leak out' in our messages through the overt and hidden metaphors, symbols and shapes we use to describe our experiences as being 'like' something else. Lakoff and Johnson (1980) suggest that the describing metaphors we use in everyday conversation are more deeply connected to our internal reality, and may present a 'truer' picture of what's going on than any conceptual language can offer. For instance, a client may continually talk about going round in circles, following a path, time running out, or being trapped 'in' a relationship. Each one of these metaphors gives you a clear sense of how the client is thinking about things and you may gain greater and deeper understanding by paying more attention to how these metaphors comes alive as they explain further. An example of this would be a client who describes their life as a 'roller coaster'. With just two words they are giving you a wealth of information about how they view their past as well as what they think about the future. They are telling you that there are exciting highs and plummeting lows and that there is only one track they can go along, and that they are going fast. Much of this understanding will be outside of the client's conscious awareness until you specifically ask about aspects of that roller coaster.

From the information above, I hope you can see that the specific language that the client uses provides many clues as to their thinking structures, which can be explored during the session(s). I strongly recommend that you undergo training in this area, whether through an NLP, clean language, systems thinking or other form of linguistic analysis and understanding.

Don't think of your next question until the client has stopped talking

I see many new coaches struggle to think up questions while the client is still talking, but by the time they are ready for the next question the issue has already shifted. Make notes, observe your intuitive reactions, then actually formulate the question once the client has stopped talking.

This has an added benefit of creating a pause in the conversation. Moments of silence separating the client's thoughts and your response are incredibly powerful. The effect for the client is very positive and supportive: the pause shows that you have listened and are completely absorbing the information before responding. Think about how it makes you feel when a person jumps in the second you stop talking with a comment or another question. Regardless of what they say, your impression is likely to be that they didn't really listen and absorb your message.

Repeating back the client's message

By repeating the client's message, it gives you a second opportunity to comprehend what it means and add a deeper level of insight. And of course it helps the client to understand more about what they mean too. After all, this could be the first time they've heard their words too. There are different ways in which you can repeat back the message, depending on your current level of understanding.

Parroting

Parroting is repeating back the client's words exactly as you heard them. This is an amazingly powerful technique and one that is used extensively within clean language. When you do nothing more than repeat those exact same words, the client feels totally listened to, honoured and understood. It also helps them to understand their own thoughts better as they hear them coming back to them from the outside. Sometimes they realize that the words are not their own, or gain some other deeper understanding of themselves through the process.

As the coach listening, for you to hear the client's words coming from their mouth and back out again from yours, will help you to internalize their message such that you are very likely to gain a deep understanding of where they are coming from – not just the message but the person behind the message, their beliefs, values and identity.

Summarizing

Here you can take the whole message that the client gave you and summarize back your understanding of the overall picture, in one short sentence. This takes some considerable skill and is best achieved by using some of the key words and expressions used by the client. Sometimes the client can be overwhelmed by the complexity of the issue they are explaining, and will value a simple overview. Be careful, however, as it is difficult to summarize without putting your own personal bias on the situation.

You could ask the client to summarize and see what they come up with. Or use some of the clean language or emergent knowledge techniques described elsewhere in this book to help the client summarize as a metaphor, shape or overall pattern. Failing that, repeating the last words that the client has given you summarizes the point that they have reached – and is likely to represent where they are right now. Often when a client gives long and complex descriptions, their understanding is shifting almost as soon as the words leave their mouth, so repeating back what they may have said five minutes previously may no longer be relevant.

Paraphrasing

Here you are forming your own understanding of what the client means and playing back that understanding using your own words and expressions. Again, you must be careful that this isn't too influenced by any personal bias. Paraphrasing presents an opportunity for you to add insight for the client, through your own intuitive interpretation of what is really going on. If you as the coach can hit upon a clear way of explaining the client's situation using different but somehow the 'right' words, then this can pave the way to new understanding for the client. There is also incredible value for the client in hearing you demonstrate that you have correctly understood them. This somehow validates their experience and in itself can be therapeutic for the client and heal past hurts/resolve unfinished business.

Time to think

Finally, in Nancy Kline's (1999) book *Time to Think*, she summarizes a simple but powerful truth, which is: 'The quality of a person's attention determines the quality of other people's thinking' (1999: 17). In fact, the very act of listening deeply and attentively can, in itself, allow a client to become wiser: 'Giving good attention to someone makes them more intelligent' (1999: 37). Remember this in your rush to help a client achieve their goals. Your ego may be encouraging you to ask that magic question, or discover that great insight, so you can bathe in the glory of the client's achievements, knowing you were instrumental in their progress. However, by 'just' listening you may unlock enough potential in the client for them to know for themselves which questions need answering and which insights needs acknowledging. And if all you do is listen, you have given the client the best gift of all – to know they are capable and have all the resources they need inside them already.

Summary

- To listen effectively you will need to fill in the gaps of your understanding in a conscious manner.
- Avoid bad listening habits and don't take listening for granted.
- Consciously work at expanding your awareness to level 3 listening.
- Prepare to listen by putting your own thoughts on hold.
- Check your understanding of the client's message by repeating it back to the client.
- Remember that when you pay exquisite attention to your client they can become wiser.

8

Questioning skills

Of all the skills employed by a life coach, questioning is the most tangible for the client. The defining moments in a coaching session are likely to be in the silence immediately after you have thought of and delivered a particularly powerful and incisive question. It's that magic moment when just the right question pops into your mind at the most useful moment, and even before that question leaves your mouth, you know it's going to make the coachee start to think differently, leading to some kind of insight. However, it is important to realize that your questioning skills, although in the 'front line', so to speak, work as part of a team. Your questions will be a direct reflection of the quality of wisdom coming from your intuition. The potency of the questions will have a close link to the level of attention you have given the client through your exquisite listening. The rapport you have formed with the coachee will ensure that they feel comfortable with being asked such powerful and profound questions by you, and they will be able to understand their meaning.

What are questions for?

As a life coach, we have a whole host of tools we could bring to a life coaching session. These tools could be physical, such as forms or psychometric tests or questionnaires that the client can touch, see, pick up and take away with them. Tools could be also be models, overall processes or theories that help us shape our coaching conversation and lead the client towards the achievement of their goal. The specific questions we ask could also be thought of as tools. And as tools, questions have a myriad of different functions and uses. Asking the right question at the right time is about recognizing what you want your question to do for the coachee right at that moment. Questions can be used to:

- relax a person and help them feel comfortable;
- open up a conversation and get the coachee to start talking;
- help you understand how the coachee thinks or feels about something;
- help the coachee gain a greater understanding of their own thoughts and feelings;
- clarify your understanding;
- check on specific facts and details;
- expand and broaden your/the coachee's focus of attention;
- narrow down the focus of attention;
- get to the nub of a specific issue;
- shift the coachee's attention to some specific facet;
- enable the coachee to connect different facets of their awareness;
- enable a decision to be made;
- get agreement on action;
- change the subject of conversation;
- encourage creative thinking about a situation;
- assess the coachee's level of commitment or motivation around taking action;
- encourage greater motivation to take action;
- offer an alternative viewpoint for consideration;
- subtly influence the coachee's opinion, belief or perception;
- reframe the coachee's opinion, belief or perception;
- challenge the coachee's opinion, belief or perception.

The last six uses will be covered in more depth in Chapter 10 ('Challenging skills') and Chapter 11 ('Motivating skills').

As you read this list of great uses for questions, I hope it helped you realize the immense potential value that is contained in every question you ask. Many questions will have multiple uses and will achieve more than one of these aims.

And the quality of your questions is far more important than the overall quantity you ask. I have witnessed some coaching practice sessions where the novice coach goes for a scattergun approach, believing that by firing enough questions at the coachee, one will hit home and achieve a result. It is better to allow the client more time to talk, and introduce your questions sparingly with a thoughtful pause beforehand.

Where do questions come from?

Questions have probably been in existence as long as language as we know it. The power of insightful questions in the coaching process was recognized as long ago as early Greek civilization, when the philosopher Socrates developed a way of asking questions that was designed to elicit wisdom and learning from the student, with the teacher feigning ignorance. Socratic questioning is still used today as a disciplined process for exploring ideas and getting to the truth. A common technique within this process is to present back a person's answer in the form of another question, leading to deeper thinking and clarification of opposing views.

So where do *your* questions come from? I have explored this question as part of a co-coaching forum, where coaches were asked to identify the source of their question, moments after they asked it. This raised a number of interesting sources of questions:

- Many coaches had listened to the client's information and formulated some strategy or approach based on the information they heard and the meaning they understood from it. For instance, one coach perceived a potential internal conflict with the client and asked a question to clarify what that conflict was. The question they asked was the start of the particular line of questioning following a learnt process or format.
- Some coaches' attention was drawn to the gaps in the information presented to them and wanted greater clarification, and they asked a question that would sharpen the

focus of the coachee, without a clear idea of what they would do next with the coachee.

- Some coaches related the coachee's statement to previous coachees and other life experience to decide on an appropriate question, sometimes drilling down for more detail, sometimes expanding out for the bigger picture, sometimes asking a question about what was missing from the client's statement.
- Some coaches felt some kind of intuitive 'knowing' about the coachee and responded with a 'curve ball' question that didn't flow naturally from the course of the conversation.

After a few hours of this approach, I began to realize that we all had fairly predictable patterns of question-choosing, which in itself is fine – we all need strategies. However, the larger the 'repository' of questions we have to pick from in the first place, the greater flexibility we will have and the more likely we will be to find just the right approach for a particular coachee.

Collecting 'great' questions somewhere in the back of your mind is very useful as they are likely to pop to the front just when you most need them. And as mentioned elsewhere, having a variety of different models and theories to inform you will lead you to explore what different questions could be asked that might take the client along a different path. It also ensures that we don't develop a blinkered 'one size fits all' approach to when selecting a question.

In the (2005) book *Good Question!*, Judy Barber explores a host of unusual and useful questions coming from all manner of sources and people. In conclusion, she says:

> I know that my best questions arise naturally in conversation. I may have used them before, borrowed them from other people or they may be new, but in a sense they are all new when they arrive fresh in the conversation, made available thoughtfully at a good moment. (2005: 244)

What defines a great question?

Julie Starr (2008: 103) suggests that there are three key elements to a great question, and I have added my interpretation of each of these elements:

- *It is simple* – the coachee has to understand it. For this reason, it must be reasonably short, and without multiple meanings or double-barrelled questions/double negatives.
- *It has a purpose* – that you have consciously recognized, even if the question popped into your head from your intuition – you have mentally checked it out and know the intention behind the question.
- *It will be influencing without being controlling* – all questions 'lead' a coachee in one direction or another. A great question invites a client to pay attention to certain aspect of their situation without making them feel forced to do something about it.

Questions to expand awareness

A well-known technique for phrasing questions in order to open up a conversation is to ask 'open questions'. Almost any kind of basic communications skills training will cover the basic structure of an open question and how to construct one. The key is generally in the first word of the question. Open questions allow the coachee to give a lot of information in return, for instance:

- 'What happened?'
- 'How do you feel about that?'
- 'Why was that?' (But be careful, 'why' questions often create a defensive response as they evoke images of blaming, criticizing parents looking to point a finger. Try 'and what are the reasons for this?' to get the answer to 'why' without the defensiveness.)

Rudyard Kipling (1902) had a rhyme for remembering open questions: 'I have six honest serving men, they serve me well and true, their names are What and How and Why and Which and When and Who'. It is important to realize, however, that the formation of the question is simply an 'invitation' to reply in a certain way and not a command that the coachee has to obey!

Often, the first answer the client gives you provides a superficial overview. By sticking with the same subject and asking further questions, you can help both you and the client build up a deeper understanding of their response and the underlying factors that may slowly rise to the surface of their consciousness:

Coach: How did you feel?
Coachee: Confident.
Coach: You felt confident. What else can you remember about that feeling of confidence?
Coachee: I felt really alive, bursting with energy.
Coach: When else have you felt that alive?
Coachee: I think it's when I know people approve of me and value what I do.
Coach: So, how do you know that people approve and value you?

Focusing in questions

A *closed* question will normally give you a yes, no or definite, single-word answer, for instance: 'Did you speak to your boss about that?'. Answer: 'Yes'. Some of Rudyard Kipling's famous six questions can be relatively closed, in that they invite a specific, one-word answer, for instance: 'When did you do that?'. Answer: 'Last Friday'.

Some open questions can help the client to narrow-down their thinking:

* What's most important out of all that?
* Which would you prefer?
* What needs to happen first?
* How would you summarize all that in just one sentence?

Adapting your question style to suit the coachee

It's worth noting that you'll have some coachees who will open up and give you lengthy responses regardless of how you ask the questions. By asking closed questions, you might get shorter, more focused answers from some coachees, but there will still be those who will expand with lots of detail. Generally, these kinds of people probably need to be given permission to express themselves expansively by sticking with open questions, at least while you begin to form a rapport.

Some coachees will give very short, non-expressive answers to your questions. In my experience, these kinds of coachees are very few and far between. It seems that once a coachee has made the decision to see a life coach, they are prepared to talk! I have had a few, however, who need some warming up to get them to open up and explain. For these kinds of people, generally using open questions should be helpful. However, if your questions are too open and non-directive, you may get a lot of 'I don't know' or 'I'm not sure' answers. Here again your one-word closed questions can begin to shape a conversation and provide you with more information to form meaningful open questions that place the coachee's attention in the areas where they are more likely to feel comfortable talking.

In general, a useful strategy to use with open and closed questions is:

- Use more open questions at the beginning of a coaching session to get a 'feel' for the coachee and their problem.
- Use more closed questions later in the session when you need precise answers and require greater control over the conversation so as to progress at the right pace, leading towards a commitment to making change and taking specific actions.

Facts or opinions?

Another way to classify questions is to ascertain, broadly speaking, what kind of information they are attempting to gain. Questions can be *fact* or *feeling* gathering. Factual questions can be useful to gain a tangible picture of the coachee's situation; 'feeling' questions will give you the subjective viewpoint – feelings, thoughts, opinions, wishes, etc. For some people you'll need to build a strong rapport before they'll feel comfortable answering some 'feeling' questions.

How do you know what to focus on?

A good start point is to question where the coachee's attention is going. Help them focus in on what they are noticing.

Conversely, at times you may direct the client's attention to the very thing they are consciously or unconsciously avoiding.

If the coachee has repeated the same word or phrase, this is usually an indication that there is more to tell about that word or phrase and you could dig a little deeper.

Are there 'gaps' in the coachee's story? See the previous chapter on listening skills for distortions, deletions and generalisations.

Is the coachee using a metaphor to describe something? The metaphor acts like a container and is likely to hold far more information than is first given. Asking questions directly about the metaphor allows the coachee to access sometimes difficult feelings and unpleasant memories in a safe way.

What is the coachee signalling unconsciously with their body language? If they shift position or give a small involuntary movement at some point it may indicate that their unconscious intuition is dropping you a hint!

And, of course, use your own intuition – see the next chapter for more on developing your intuitive skills.

Questioning processes

I am now going to highlight three specific questioning processes that I find particularly useful for life coaching.

Clean language

As we covered earlier, clean language is a process that consists of a set of questions to ask, normally focused on the coachee's descriptive metaphors. Clean language can bring about extraordinary results by enabling the coachee to go deeper into their own thoughts, habits and perceptions, where they find their own unique solutions. The 'deepness' of thinking is enhanced by asking clean questions of the metaphoric content of the coachee's communication. This focuses their attention on the *structure* of their thinking and experience, rather than the same old problem-content that they've thought in the same old way many times before.

Metaphors are increasingly recognized not simply as a communication device, but as fundamental to human thinking (Lakoff and Johnson, 1980). When a person describes their experience using a descriptive metaphor, it holds the key to *how* they are thinking about that experience. By exploring the metaphor that an individual naturally uses (often subconsciously), you can help enable understanding at a core level – often resulting in transformational change. When a coachee begins to pay attention to the metaphor that they are using, the symbols, shapes and elements of that metaphor often 'come to life'. Then, as the coachee learns more about their own internal 'symbolic landscape', the session becomes like a guided visualization but with the client being their own guide.

Change can happen simply, for example when the client becomes aware of a previously unnoticed resource that enables their metaphors to shift or evolve in some way. Change can also happen spontaneously, emerging as a function of the exploration process. Or change may be the result of the coachee being facilitated to 'self-model' their binding patterns; how these are structured and how they replicate. As metaphors change in relation to the client's desired outcome, their perception of the problem changes as well. The coach's chief role is to direct the client's attention to different parts of their experience, and here is where the skill lies – knowing where to focus attention.

The process also involves asking questions in a certain way, using a special repetitive syntax:

- And . . . [repeat coachee's words].
- And when [zone in on a specific part of what the coachee has said],
- [Ask a clean language question].

This repetition of the coachee's actual words is like holding a mirror up to the coachee, so that they see themselves reflected back through their own words, descriptions and metaphors. This becomes mesmerizing and coachees tend to go into a very deep state of self-reflective relaxation, like a light 'trance'. Although far from being asleep, clients stay highly alert and participative during the process.

Examples of clean language questions
Coachee: 'I'd like to choose the right path for my future career'. You could say: 'And you'd like to choose the right path for your future career.' [Pause] 'And when you'd like to choose the right path (for your future career)' . . .

- 'What kind of path is that path?'
- 'Is there anything else about that path?'
- 'Whereabouts is that path?'
- 'What kind of future career is that future career?'
- 'Is there anything else about "choose"?'
- 'What happens next?'

With clean language, what you wouldn't do is:

- assume a potential solution, e.g. 'So how do you feel about retraining?'
- suggest a direction to take, e.g. 'So what happens if you choose the quickest and easiest path?'
- introduce other metaphors of your own, e.g. 'What vehicle could help you along this path?'

What being 'clean' involves
Being clean involves:

- mirroring back the coachee's words and metaphors to the coachee;
- being non-judgemental and flexible;
- keeping yourself out of the coachee's picture;
- recognizing and understanding your own metaphors and how they influence you and your thinking;
- being in rapport with the coachee's metaphors rather than the coachee themselves;
- holding your own opinions 'lightly' and letting them go in favour of new information.

The basic clean language question set and the purpose of each

- *To find out what the coachee wants*: 'And what would you like to have happen?'
- *To gain more detail*: 'What kind of [coachee's words] is that [coachee's words]?'

- *To find out where the symbols and metaphors are, to locate them in space*, e.g. inside the head, heart, floating above, etc: 'Whereabouts is [coachee's words]?'
- *To expand further awareness*: 'And is there anything else about [coachee's words]?'
- *To bring about a clearer form*: 'And does [coachee's words] have a shape or a size?'
- *To encourage a metaphoric description*: 'That's [coachee's words] like what?'
- *To explore time sequence – by moving forwards in time*: 'Then what happens?'
- *To explore time sequence – by moving backwards in time*: 'What happened just before?'
- *To get right back to the original source of something*: 'Where could [coachee's words] have come from?'
- *To explore relationships and connections*: 'And is there a relationship between [coachee's words "x"] and [client's words "y")?' *or* 'And when [client's words], what happens to [coachee's words]?'
- *To find out how a goal can be reached*: 'What needs to happen for [coachee's goal]?' *and* 'And can [coachee's words]?'

Exercise: Using clean language to have a greater connection with a positive resource or feeling you have
What would you like more of in your life? Choose a feeling/ state of mind or quality, for instance:

- happiness;
- a positive attitude;
- calmness; or
- any other quality.

Then read and answer this question: 'And when you would like more "xxxx" in your life, is there anything else about that "xxxx"?'. Write down your answer:

Now write down three clean language questions you could ask next of what you've written:

2

3

Then spend some time answering these questions in writing, in as much detail as you can. If you have a coach partner that would like to practice this with you, you could take it in turns to share the answers, then ask further clean language questions, paying particular attention to any metaphors that you have used.

Appreciative inquiry

This is an organizational development approach to problem solving that works by focusing on what's working and finding out how to have more of that. It fits nicely with the solution-focused, non-directive approach used by most life coaches. It follows a four-step process, which is outlined below along with example questions for each step:

- *discovery* – appreciating and valuing the best of 'what is'
  - 'What do you have in your life at the moment for which you are truly grateful?'
  - 'What do you value most about yourself?'
  - 'Can you think of a time that you felt extremely confident. What was happening at the time? What circumstances led to your confident state of mind?'
- *dream* – envisioning 'what might be' by exploring possibilities for the future, based on past achievements
  - 'What could be possible if you always felt that confident?'
  - 'What would happen if all that you value most in yourself could be expressed fully?'
  - 'From your past successes, what best possible outcome could the future hold?'
  - 'And what other possibilities can you envision?'
- *design* – dialoguing 'what should be' by setting goals based on the most compelling ideas that come from the 'dream' stage
  - 'What kind of future do you want?'
  - 'Where would you like to be, five years from now?'

     ❍ 'What principles do you need to follow to reach that goal?'
- *delivery* – innovating 'what will be' by setting achievable actions
     ❍ 'How can you make this goal a reality?'
     ❍ 'What steps do you need to take to make this happen?

Most importantly, appreciative inquiry questions are always directed at the positive part of whatever the client describes.

Emergent knowledge

As introduced in Chapter 4, this is a new methodology to coaching that was created by David Grove in the last few years of his life. Based on the scientific principles of emergence and 'small world' networks, it works by having the client 'connect the dots' of all known information in such a way that a clearer and simpler higher-level understanding can emerge. The process works by asking the same kind of question around six times. Each time the question is asked it is recursive, i.e. asked of the next piece of information the coachee has just given you. The effect is like peeling back layers of an onion skin, each answer getting deeper and deeper into the coachee. And more than that, as each answer is spoken, it connects to all the others. Grove's theory was that after asking around six questions about the same thing, the coachee has six different 'points' of information all interconnected to now form a network – which is then capable of forming a different kind of answer – the 'whole' becomes greater than the sum of the parts. The success of this technique is in creating the right starting conditions for the different areas of knowledge to begin emerging from the coachee's unconsciousness:

Questions to create a 'clean' start:
Write down or draw your goal (or even pick an object that could represent it) on a piece of paper, and place that paper (or object) where it needs to be, somewhere in the space around you. Then, place yourself where you need to be in relation to that goal. This may seem like an odd thing to do, however I

have not yet met a client who doesn't understand what's required here. The client will create a special representation of however they are perceiving the distance between themselves and the goal they wish to achieve. Some will place the goal far away, some nearby. Some up high, some low. And some will hide it. All will have some special significance for the client and help them to understand how they currently see the goal and the journey they need to make to get there.

This basic 'set-up' is then more finely tuned by asking a series of check questions along the following lines:

- And is the goal in the right space?
- And is it at the right height?
- And is it at the right angle?
- And are you in the right position?
- And are you facing the right direction?
- And is the distance right between you and your goal?

Again, in my experience, most coachees have little trouble understanding the questions and start to fine-tune the position of the goal and themselves in relation to it. All the while, the coachee is paying exquisite attention to something they have probably not thought of before. Rather than focusing on the specific content of the goal, they are focusing on the unique relationship between the two points in their imagination, made real and tangible by laying them out in the space before them. Many coachees get new insights just by going through a clean start as described here.

Getting outside the 'small world' network of A, B and C

As covered in Chapter 4, a client is usually seeking to get from A to B when they come to a coach. If C represents everything that exists in the coachee's mind between A and B, then it is likely to contain whatever is stopping them achieving B. So, any kind of thinking that is focused on A, B or C is likely to reinforce the 'small world' network that is stuck within a problem scenario. By asking questions to get information that is *adjacent* to the known information, the coach's goal is to have the coachee ultimately break free from this small world, and gain insights that come from outside of this network.

Networking what, not who you know

After the 'clean start', the coach would ask a series of questions, most of which begin with 'And what do you know?', then 'And what else do you know?'. Sometimes the coachee is asked to move location or position after each knowledge collection, sometimes the client is asked to focus on a particular word or letter within the goal they have written down.

All the techniques are simply ways to have the coachee think around the same thing six times. At the end of six questions, the coach would ask: 'And what do you know now?'. The piling on of layers of information serves to create a complex neural network that eventually gets overloaded with detail. Once that happens the coachee's understanding is likely to shift as a higher-level perspective emerges. The final question serves to summarize the new understanding. This process could continue with numerous rounds of six questions or a coach could move into a more traditional coaching approach.

What if you don't know what question to ask next?

I have compiled here a short list of very useful questions to keep up your sleeve in case of emergency. These questions will work well in any scenario when you may feel 'stuck' and are not quite sure what to ask next. Each question has the effect of putting the client in the driving seat and deciding for themselves how best the coaching session should proceed. As with any question, they will be more effective if you have been really listening to the coachee and have built up a sufficient rapport.

• What question could I ask you right now that would be most useful for you to explore?
• What question are you secretly hoping that I won't ask you, yet you know will lead you to new insights, if asked?
• Imagine years from now, this goal has been achieved and then some, and as you look back from the future and remember this session you realize that the turning point for you happened at this very moment. What was the question I asked you that made the difference?

- Just suppose, that everything in your life has happened and will happen just as it should, all for your best interests. Everything happens for a reason and even negative happenings have an eventual positive outcome. If that were so, what could be the positive intention behind your problem here?
- What if you were the coach, and I were the client? Imagine I have just explained to you exactly what you've told me. What question would you, as the coach, ask next?

Summary

- Questions are at the 'front end' of your skills, but work as part of a team alongside your listening, relationship-building and intuitive skills.
- Consider the purpose of your question and phrase it accordingly.
- The larger your repository of questions, the greater your flexibility in choosing the most appropriate question.
- As well as having a clear purpose, great questions are also simple, and designed to influence without controlling the client.
- Use appropriate questions to expand awareness and/or focus attention, depending on where you are in the coaching process and the kind of client you are working with.
- There are a variety of coaching questioning methodologies you can learn that provide an overall structure and shape to your questioning strategy.
- It is useful to have a few universal coaching questions up your sleeve in case you/the coachee gets 'stuck' at any point in the session.

9

Intuitive skills

What I say is more often felt through intuition than
thought through intellect.

Albert Einstein (Hermanns, 1983: 55)

Defining intuition

What is intuition? The generally held definition is *the ability
to understand or know something immediately, without conscious reasoning.* The word originally comes from the Latin
word *intuērī*, meaning simply 'to look at'. Over the years,
the word and the meaning developed into the Middle English
word 'intuicioun', meaning 'insight' or 'to see within', which
has a closer connection with our modern understanding of
the word. However, later in this chapter I will highlight that
insight and intuition are not necessarily the same thing.

Intuition involves access to our own inner repository
of knowledge stored in the unconscious part of our brain.
It is constantly being fed by all the information collected
consciously and unconsciously through our five senses, all
subreferenced to every other piece of information we have
collected during our lives. Recent research backs up the fact
that although intuitive thoughts may appear to come 'out of
the blue', they are in fact the result of the way our brains
store, process and retrieve information on a non-conscious
level (Hodgkinson *et al.*, 2008):

It is no wonder, then, that our unconsciousness is so
much wiser than our consciousness.

Jung (1992) described intuition as one of the four possible

dimensions to how people perceive the world around them. In this early model of the personal psyche, *intuition* was opposed by *sensation* on one axis, while *feeling* was opposed by *thinking* on another axis. Jung argued that, in a given individual, one of these four functions was primary (most prominent or developed) in the consciousness. Sensory people know things by what they see, hear or touch, and they have proof to back up their knowledge; intuitive people simply know. Later, however, we will explore how using our conscious ability to more accurately sense the world around us seems to result in improvement in our intuitive skills, in the opposite dimension.

The elusive 'locked door'

Some coaches seem to have an uncanny 'knack' of knowing what's going on with the client and where to focus attention. Where does that intuition come from? How can we improve our 'gut feeling' if it resides somewhere outside of our consciousness? These are some of the many questions about intuition I have considered in order to discover how it can be harnessed most effectively by a coach. These questions were explored in depth at one of our recent co-coaching forums, initially to discover how important the group felt their intuition was, in guiding their choice of questions. All coaches felt it was a vital attribute for a coach. However, when the group were questioned on how they actually access their intuition, it became clear that there was no hard-and-fast rule. Most didn't really understand how their intuition worked and many were reluctant to try and find out. By trusting their intuition implicitly, it worked for them, and there was a concern that by trying to dissect what was actually happening at a deeper, unconscious level, it might somehow prevent it from working in the future.

Can you think of a time when you have just instantly known something without being told or learning it cognitively? It may have been some profound understanding of a person, or simply a certainty of something that was about to happen. These flashes of intuition become significant when we later discover the facts that confirm that our intuition was accurate. But this leaves us with the question: 'How did I know I knew?'

The bestselling book *Blink* by Malcolm Gladwell (2005) was based around the 'power of thinking without thinking', and Gladwell references many examples of how intuition has been used by people to access an instant impression of something that proves to be accurate. He calls the process of intuition *thin slicing*: 'The ability of our unconscious to find patterns in situations and behaviour based on very narrow slices of experience' (2005: 23). He goes on to give examples of its elusive nature and says:

> If we are to learn to improve the quality of the decisions we make, we need to accept the mysterious nature of our snap judgements. We need to respect the fact that it is possible to know without knowing why we know and accept that – sometimes – we're better off that way.
>
> (2005: 23)

As intuition is a function seemingly controlled by our unconscious mind, the 'not knowing' could be an unavoidable aspect of this skill. That doesn't mean that we can absolve ourselves of all responsibility to develop our intuition, as there are many conscious skills we can practice and hone, which in turn will strengthen our intuitive ability.

Developing skills to enhance your intuition

Sensory acuity

'Sensory acuity' is a term from NLP that means developing your observational skills to notice the subtle changes that may take place in a client's physiology that alerts you to a change in state:

> Sensory acuity involves paying greater attention to the information you get through your senses. The more you pay attention, the great your discriminating ability, the finer detail you can gather, and the more you can make comparisons between different sorts and degrees of information.
>
> (McDermott and Jago, 2001: 76)

There are some very prescriptive processes within the field of NLP, such as deducing what kind of thinking is going on by eye movements and gaze direction. More important than any standardized 'meanings' is to notice the particular body language and verbal clues that the client gives you that may reveal more about what is going on for them internally. The NLP skill of matching a client's body language to what they are thinking is called 'calibration'. When the client tells you they are feeling really happy, and they sound and look happy, take a note of what the client's physiology is telling you. So, when you notice these same signals again in the client, you can associate them with the client's likely feelings of happiness.

There are some common clues and signals you can watch for: *eye gaze* is a significant one. Where does the client look before they tell you how they really feel? Where do they look after you ask a particularly challenging question? Over time you can begin to notice a pattern of what these different eye gazes may mean.

Facial expression is another one. Different 'looks' flash momentarily across a person's face, reflecting what they are feeling inside. Various studies have shown that a myriad of complex emotions are encoded in our facial expressions and can be accurately deciphered by freeze-framing a video and analysing the position and movement of facial muscles:

> Whenever we experience a basic emotion, that emotion
> is automatically expressed by the muscles of the face.
> That response may linger on the face for just a faction
> of a second or be detectable only if electrical sensors
> are attached to the face. But it's always there.
>
> (Gladwell, 2005: 210)

The *body position* of the client is another big clue as to something subtly shifting. Notice the position of their shoulders and whether they are leaning forwards or backwards, whether the chin is up or down. Shifts in energy and motivation are likely to alter these outline views. One NLP practice exercise I did during my training involved a demonstration subject who stood at the front of the class and was asked a series of questions. The facilitator asked the demonstration subject to initially tell the truth in answering all the questions, so that we could 'calibrate' the body language and voice clues to this person's 'truthful' answer. The facilitator then asked the demonstration subject to purposely lie in answering the same set of questions, and once again we were asked to calibrate, noticing the subtle differences that occurred in the body and voice when the person was lying. The facilitator then asked the demonstration subject some new questions, which they could choose whether to answer truthfully or otherwise. After our initial calibration session we all found it easy to spot whether the demonstration subject was telling the truth or lying. What was even more fascinating was when the demonstration subject was asked to turn their back on us and repeat with a new set of questions. Without seeing the face, just noticing body shifts and voice we were still all able to identify a truth or a lie. You can play this game at home!

Twitches or tics are another signal – the client's subconscious is 'flagging' something that you should pay attention to. An example of this in action could be the client who, whenever they mention their mother, twists their wrist slightly. The point here is not to try and work out why this happens or even to mention it to the client, but just to notice the signal and what it seems to relate to. Later, when they are referring to their new boss, and they twist their wrist, you may draw the conclusion that they are thinking of their mother again on some level. The question you decide to ask, to check out this information, could be. 'I'm just wondering, is there anything about your new boss that reminds you of your mother?'. Please notice that this is a closed question on purpose. We want the client to feel perfectly able to say 'No' as sometimes we will get these signals wrong and we need to check them out with the client in a respectful way.

Skin tone/colour and shine is another interesting change to watch out for. It is surprising how quickly it can change and 'give away' a client's thoughts. Blushing is, of course, one we all know and are aware of, but there are subtle skin appearance shifts that you can look out for too.

When to pay attention to sensory acuity

What happens just before the client answers your question? Pay attention at that moment to what is happening and you will learn about the clues and cues that this person unconsciously gives you about their innermost thoughts. What shifts or changes in the client as they speak? Notice what is being mentioned when the shift occurs. The more you practice and develop sensory acuity on a conscious level, the more you will train your brain to operate this way on an unconscious level, when you no longer have to work at this, and it will just happen automatically.

Inner senses as well as outer senses

Remember we have five senses that we use to inform us of what is going on with a client. All the sensory examples given are mainly using the visual or auditory senses. But what if our sense of smell is able to discern between the subtle chemicals emanating from different emotions or feelings? We know that many animals have a highly developed sense of smell, and maybe we do too, but because of our highly developed cognitive ability we have 'forgotten' about it. But perhaps it still functions and feeds our intuition, unconsciously.

And what about touch? Do we pick up on the subtle energy vibrations that come from the client? Many people believe this but it is yet to be proved. You have probably experienced the unnerving sensation of shivers down your spine, or someone 'walking over your grave'. Could this be your unconsciousness alerting you to pay attention to something? In the book *Discovering the Body's Wisdom*, Mirka Knaster (1996) suggests that this is indeed the case, explaining how the 'inner' senses of proprioception (awareness of the precise position of our body) and kinesthesia (awareness of direction of movement) allow us to know where we are in space and time and together work as a sixth sense. Through this sixth sense, Knaster suggests that we pick up the energy emanating from others: 'We sense this energy as subtle vibrations from others – almost like sound waves lapping at the shore of our bodies' (1996: 59).

Notice what *all* your body is telling you about the client, not just your eyes and ears.

Developing your conscious knowledge

The more we continue to learn and increase our conscious knowledge with up-to-date, accurate facts, theories and models, the bigger and more wide-reaching our internal repository of information will be. This provides the raw material that our unconscious can draw on. In the book *How the Mind Works* Stephen Pinker (1997) explains how we are all expert 'pattern spotters' and compare and contrast what we our noticing out there with the previously stored information 'boxes', with categories and subcategories, rules and exceptions: 'Intelligence does not come from a special kind of spirit or matter or energy but from a different commodity, information' (1997: 65).

Accessing your intuition and voicing the message

Some people are better than others at spotting the intuitive 'itch' coming from somewhere inside themselves. Practice paying attention to your body as well as your head during a coaching session, tune into what thoughts and feelings bubble up and recognise their significance. By voicing these intuitive ideas we can learn whether they do contain wisdom – or not – as the case may be: 'We develop our access to intuition in the same way we develop talents or muscles' (Whitworth *et al.*, 2007: 58). Each time we verbalize them we can receive feedback, learning how to fine-tune our interpretations and what might need filtering out.

How you communicate it to the client

Although it is important to acknowledge the intuitive spark and analyze it consciously for a moment or two, the 'flash of light is already beginning to fade as soon as it appears' (Whitworth *et al.*, 2007: 59). So speak up about it quickly, before the moment – and your sense of what it might mean – passes away.

Holding the intuitive thought lightly

Voice your thoughts out loud and check the client's reaction. It will not always be right, and that's still okay as often something else will arise from an inaccurate intuitive comment you raise. For example, the client may say 'No, that's not what's happening. But now I think I know what is . . .'. If the client does not feel that your intuitive thought is significant, be prepared to let it go and move on.

Utilising the client's own intuition

As well as tuning in to your own intuition, remember to look out for the client's subtle signals that their intuition is informing them of something. Some questions (particularly using emergent knowledge techniques) may be asked specifically to help the client access their own inner wisdom.

Trusting your intuition

This is not a skill but an essential belief that will develop over time. As your inklings prove to be wise, your confidence in them will increase.

The difference between instinct, intuition and insight

Instinct is our inherent, unlearned pattern of responses, for instance a fight or flight reaction to a dangerous situation. Our instinct could also be feeding into our intuition on some level. Rather than a clearly formed thought, our instinct is likely to present us with a sensation or feeling, or a strong desire to attack or run away.

To contrast intuition with insight, David Perkins (2002: unpaginated) offers this comparison:

> It's worth examining how intuition contrasts with insight, since the two terms often go together. What's the difference between calling something an intuition and calling something an insight?

To call an idea an intuition is to say how you got to it – you got to it without having conscious reasons.

To call an idea an insight is to say that it was valuable in a certain way – 'This insight really remade the way I thought about such and such.'

In other words, intuition has to do with the path by which you arrive at an idea – without conscious reasons. Insight has to do with the importance of the idea in remaking the way you see things.

It is only with the benefit of hindsight can we learn whether our intuitive thought is also insightful. I don't believe anyone will get it right all the time, however with increased awareness and practice we can strengthen the correlation between the two.

Exercises to improve your intuitive skills

Intuition is a great skill that needs much practice and perseverance in order to use it elegantly and confidently with a client. Fortunately, we can practise noticing the clues in any conversation we are observing or joining in with. Initially, this may just be about getting used to noticing the signals without trying to understand what they might mean. When you have sharpened your ability to notice, then you can practise the following exercises with a friend or co-coaching colleague.

Exercise 1: Developing sensory acuity

Ask your friend to describe a room in the house they lived in as a child. Notice where their eyes go to access the memory of the room. Notice if any feelings are evoked, what physiological clues seem to be transmitted.

Now ask your friend to describe two situations: (a) a happy memory; (b) a nervous memory. Again notice the clues. You could add in a third one, drawing in the feeling the first exercise evoked and notice if the clues are the same.

Now ask your friend to think about either a happy or a nervous memory, but not to tell you which it is. Ask them a couple of questions to help the client access the memory but without them saying anything to you to give the game away:

- 'How old were you?'
- 'Were other people present?'
- 'Were you indoors or outside?'

After three questions, see if you can identify whether your friend is thinking of a happy or a nervous memory.

Exercise 2: Noticing your inner senses

This exercise is to help you notice your own personal intuitive 'signal', trust it and practice voicing it in a comfortable way for the client. Again, work with a friend or colleague who knows that your intention is to practice your intuitive skills. Ask your friend or colleague to share with you a current problem or difficulty that they are having. Keep the conversation going by asking questions. However, pay attention to your own body/head/space around you during the conversation. Whenever you notice any shifts or 'nudges', raise your hand to let your colleague know, who at that point will pause. You can then express whatever is going on for you and see if there is any significance for the 'client'.

This exercise is likely to produce some odd questions such as: 'Wait, I just felt an itch in my big toe and at the same time an image of an astronaut popped into my head. Does that mean anything to you?' What you are looking for is the internal feeling and pictures that seem to have some connection to the client's situation. See if the accurate intuitions are coming from the same place, somewhere inside of you.

Exercise 3: Develop a greater understanding of your intuition

This is an exercise using clean language and symbolic modelling to help you get a clearer sense of the process of intuitive insight for you. Ideally, you should have a skilled coach ask you the following statements/questions. Otherwise you can read them out yourself:

- Think of a time that you felt really intuitive.
- Describe what happened and how you felt.
- What kind of intuition was that intuition?
- And whereabouts is that intuition?
- Does that intuition have a shape or a size?
- Can you create a symbol or a metaphor that describes what all of that intuition is like for you?
- Draw it.
- And what happens just before that intuition? What happens next? Then what happens?
- What do you know now about your intuition that you didn't know before?
- And what difference does that knowing make?

After this exercise, you may want to set up a little reminder to help you remember to 'switch on' (or find another more suitable metaphor to describe what happens for you) your intuition skills at the start of each client session. You may want to somehow represent your symbol or metaphor in your practice room. When *I'm* being intuitive I am like a lighthouse, with a 360-degree awareness all around me. I have a picture of a lighthouse on the front of the notebook I use when I am with clients.

Exercise 4: Meditation

Our mental chatter with its constant stream of conscious thoughts is a distraction to what might be going on at a deeper unconscious level. Any form of meditation will help us to let go of the conscious thoughts and notice what might pop up instead without placing any significance or relevance on them. Meditation trains the brain to access the unconscious and the more you practice in a meditative state, the easier it will become for you to access this whenever and wherever you need to.

A very simple meditation exercise is to pick some object to focus all your attention onto. Take some deep breaths and let yourself relax, looking at the object and letting your normal, everyday, mental chatter fade until you can notice single thoughts, feelings and sensations as they float by your consciousness and off into the void again. Practise this every day for about five minutes, and record afterwards whatever came to mind. Over time, patterns may emerge that hold significance for you.

Summary

Although intuition is an elusive, unconscious ability, you can enhance your intuition by:
- consciously improving your sensory acuity;
- paying attention to what happens when you have an intuitive 'nudge'
  - internally within you
  - externally with the client;
- paying attention to what happens when you voice your intuitive thought;
- valuing your intuition as a critical skill that shapes your overall coaching ability.
- trusting your inner wisdom and being happy to express what it tells you (but, being prepared to let it go if on occasions it is wrong).

10

Challenging skills

Effective challenge is an extra beneficial dimension that you can bring to the coach–client relationship. A challenge is when you give the client feedback that presents them with an alternative viewpoint. Ideally, you will offer this viewpoint by way of a question, or by simply stating the facts about what you are noticing. Occasionally, you may feel it appropriate to express your feelings and opinions about it too. If that is the case, always ask for the client's permission: 'May I offer you some feedback here based on my perception of the situation and what I think?'

The difference between objective and subjective feedback

Sometimes you will give objective feedback, where you just reflect back what you are noticing – only the facts. Sometimes your feedback will be subjective, where you give not only the facts but also your subjective interpretation or opinion of those facts. It's okay to use a mix of objective and subjective feedback, so long as you are clear on which you are using and for what purpose (Starr, 2008: 129).

The right and wrong kind of challenge

The right kind of challenging helps the client recognise the difference between what they think they are doing and what other people may be perceiving about them. It helps them see any incongruence between their goals and their actions or their values and their behaviours. In short, challenging holds a mirror to the client and reflects back the whole person, including any blind spots and missing pieces of perception.

The wrong kind of challenge is one that comes from a desire in you to 'fix' the client, or a challenge that has surfaced as a result of some kind of sore spot being triggered in you. These kinds of challenges are usually heard as 'criticisms' and rarely result in a change of attitude or behaviour. They are more likely to result in an entrenchment of views as the client finds ways to defend themselves, building up an argument of justification, and preventing any opportunity to change perspective.

Hint – if you are feeling emotional about it, it is probably coming from a personal issue or desire, rather than anything to do with the client. In this situation, rather than challenge with a statement of fact or opinion, or even a question, which may come out too 'loaded', you may take it as an intuitive signal and offer it to the client for comment. For example: 'As you expressed your feelings about Bruce just then, I felt a real sense of sadness inside me. I just wondered if I was picking up on something going on for you there, or is it just my own feeling?'

A challenge could also be an action-based challenge. For instance, you could 'challenge' the client to try something, or take an action, before you meet again. This kind of challenging can work if the client feels motivated enough to stretch themselves (for more on this, see Chapter 11: 'Motivating skills').

To be skilled in the art of challenging requires an assertive mindset, courage, confidence and conviction in your own views and opinions. It also requires an empathic ability to value the client; their right to see things their own way, including their right to be wrong. You need to be able to avoid an aggressive or submissive response by carefully timing your challenge, bringing it to the client's attention and vocalizing the message clearly enough that the client can understand what you mean without it causing offence or resentment.

Challenging assertively

Assertiveness is an attitude of mind that first and foremost acknowledges equal rights. The client has the right to ignore your feedback. You have a right (in fact a duty) to inform the client. Getting your attitude right before you challenge helps you to deliver the message 'on the level' and not talk down to the client, or appear overly 'soft'.

The five steps to phrasing an assertive, challenging statement are as follows:

1 *Actively listen and show your understanding of the client's viewpoint first*: 'I can understand why you reacted as you did, and no wonder you were angry.'
2 *State the facts – according to what you can see and hear*: 'What I can see now is a look of regret on your face.'
3 *Own your opinion by stating your views on this, starting with 'I think. . .'*: 'I wonder if a different response may have helped Mary to understand you without feeling intimidated by your anger.'
4 *Explain further what you see are the wider consequences and considerations*: 'By getting mad, you make it easy for Mary to avoid talking to you in the future, which will only make matters worse.'
5 *Ask the coachee for their response: 'What do you think?'*: 'Can you think of other ways you could respond in the future that might get Mary on your side?'

Discrepancy assertion

This is an assertive technique you can use when you are hearing conflicting statements from the client. It may be you are hearing two different versions of a situation, or two contrasting beliefs or values. With this technique, you endeavour to be as objective as possible, presenting clearly back to the client the two conflicting pieces of information and simply asking for clarification. For example: 'I'm a little confused. Earlier you said that you had told Jack you wanted to move house, however just now you have said that you must find a way of telling Jack how you feel about moving. Can you clarify for me where you are with this?'. Or: 'I'm curious. In the last session you explained how important you felt that it was to tell the truth at all times, yet now you are planning to lie to Jack. How does that sit with your value around telling the truth?'

Transactional analysis and challenge

The 'transactional analysis' psychological approach (Berne, 1967) is a useful framework to understand when you are challenging. Transactional analysis was developed by Dr Eric Berne in the late 1960s and has grown into its own branch of psychotherapy. Its basic aim is to provide a user-friendly model to understand human relationships and interactions. Berne explains that human communications are a series of 'transactions' that can be viewed as games, as there are winners, losers or pay-offs. A client may unconsciously play a 'game' with you, pressing your 'buttons' to behave in a certain way that achieves a certain outcome for the client. This unconscious outcome may not be a positive one; it is more likely to reaffirm a certain negative belief that they have about themselves or other people: 'See, I knew he couldn't be trusted' – the 'pay-off' then becomes 'I'm right not to be trusting'.

Berne uses the terms *child*, *adult* and *parent* to describe three different identities we all have within us, from which we perceive the world and respond to it.

Child identity

The first identity we develop in our lives is, of course, that of a *child*. As babies and young children we have a simplistic view of ourselves and the world around us, with a few but very powerful needs and four key overriding emotions: sadness, happiness, fear and anger. As a *'natural child'* we are curious, playful, 'raw' and creative.

The child personality has two alternative facets that the child learns as they grow a bit older, both as a result of adapting to their environment. The first is the *compliant child*. As the child begins to realize that they exist as a separate identity to their parents, they become aware of their own dependence. They learn that if they don't behave they will not get ice cream. They hear 'don't run', 'stop', 'be quiet or else. . .'. The compliant child does as they are told and cries for attention. The compliant child asks for help, is totally helpless themselves. When a client is 'stuck' in this kind of identity they will come across as victims, never in control of their lives and always being made to do things by other people. The second 'adapted' identity is the *rebellious child*, and every parent will know the kind of thought processes and behaviours that are universal to that identity. The rebellious child will say 'No!' and 'You can't make me'. They stamp their feet and put their hands on their hips. They do the opposite of what you expect, not because they want to particularly, rather their motivation is to be contrary, because they now have learnt that they can and want to push out their – and your – boundaries.

Adult identity

When we are still children, our basic '*adult*' identity begins to form (at around 30 months of age). This side of ourselves is the one we like to think we always are. Rational, logical, living in the here and now, and not ruled by our emotions.

Parent identity

The final identity we have has two facets – the *nurturing parent* and the *critical parent*.

Our personal versions of these identities are likely to closely reflect our own parents' attitudes and behaviours towards us when we were children.

The *nurturing parent* is the caring, sympathetic side, helping others, supportive and kind. An overdeveloped nurturing parent will result in a person who has the habit of 'rescuing' others – usually victims, setting up a kind of 'game' where both will be getting their unconscious desires met within a dysfunctional relationship.

The other parental side is that of the *critical parent*. This identity is blaming, judgemental and bossy. They order you, tell you off and, of course, criticise. They say 'You should...', 'You must...', 'You will...' and 'or else'. The body language is towering over and looking down at, usually over the top of the glasses. You'll see lots of finger pointing and pursed lips.

The danger in a coach–client relationship is that some kind of parent–child relationship develops, especially when we are challenging. When you offer empathy and understanding, the client feels rescued, confirming to them that they are not capable of coping 'on their own'. When you challenge, if you are not careful, the message will 'speak' to the client's child, awakening either a defiant 'No way' or a weak 'I'll try'. Compliant child and rebellious child really are two sides of the same coin: someone who appears compliant and says 'Yes, I'm really sorry and I really will try harder next time' may have a deeper voice saying 'I'll show you...'.

The key to transactional analysis is to understand that we trigger certain identities or 'ego states' in another person by our own behaviours. So, we can encourage an 'adult' response by talking to the other person as though they were completely and fully in their adult state. We also need to be super-sensitive to our own switching ego states, and stay firmly in our 'adult' regardless of what the client may trigger in us. Be persistent, as when a client falls into a child or parent ego state, if you continue to talk to their adult from yours, that part of their personality will 'wake up' and play ball eventually.

Knowing when to challenge

Timing is crucial when challenging a client. It is important to understand where the client is in terms of their willingness to listen and openness to your challenge. Catching them in their 'adult' ego state means that they are less likely to be defensive or aggressive about your comment.

Ensuring that you take the time to build a good, healthy rapport between you and the client will help them understand your message and want to appreciate where you are coming from.

What to challenge a client about

The following are some of the different things you may notice about the client that require you to challenge.

Blind spot

A blind spot is something the client has no idea about themselves but you can see that it is negatively affecting their ability to reach their goals. For example, you can clearly see that the client is making no effort in their appearance, hair and clothes, yet they don't see this as being anything to do with the fact that they never seem to meet potential romantic partners. Try for yourself to phrase a coaching conversation to address this, using the five-step assertive approach described earlier in this chapter.

Sore spot

This is something that the client already recognizes is an issue or a problem to them. However they are minimizing it and downplaying its effect, misleading themselves by pretending it's not (or no longer) a problem. For example, this could be something like an issue with losing their temper. The client has told you that this used to be a problem for them, but now they recognize the warning signs and 'walk away' when things are getting potentially heated. Reading in between the lines, you think you are hearing signs that this person is once more allowing their temper to get the better of them, although they are keen to tell you that they have remained calm. If you raise it there is a danger that they will be oversensitive and take your comment to heart.

Timing is important as well as careful delivery of the message. By phrasing the message as a question you can help the client come to terms with the possibility in a gentle way before voicing your opinion (if necessary). You might say, for example: 'I'm interested in how that conversation yesterday went. It sounds as though Mary got upset, from what you have described. What was happening in the moments before she got upset? How did your comments impact on her, do you think? How would you describe your tone of voice during that conversation? How do you think Mary would describe it?'

Misaligned values

This is where the client tells you that something is very important to them, yet you are hearing over and over again that they are not valuing this thing in their lives currently. So, for example, the client keeps telling you how important it is that they spend as much quality time with their family as they can, however what you hear is that as soon as they have some free time, they race off to the golf club/gym. Here you need to present the client with the two pieces of information – the values you are hearing versus the behaviour. You can ask the client for more information to explain the seeming inconsistency.

Projection

Projection is where the client notices fault in other people that reflects what they don't like in themselves and they fail to notice consciously that they have this same trait. A good way to challenge this is to ask the client to put themselves in another person's shoes and describe what they see from that perspective. The other way you could do this is to get the client to list those specific behaviours that lead them to conclude that a certain person has this negative trait. And then ask the client to notice when they themselves could have displayed those behaviours themselves. Be prepared to describe specific scenarios that they have explored with you and throw in some potential different perspectives as 'food for thought'.

Victim

The victim is the client who continually fails to move forwards because something 'happens', out of their control and outside of their own action and behaviour. This is a tricky one as if you are not careful they will pull the 'victim' game on you and make you their 'persecutor', for pointing out their inability to take responsibility. Or they make you the 'rescuer', so that you become the only one who can save them by telling them what to do. Challenge them gently by exploring other actions they could take if they were in control.

Optimist

The optimist is the client who is overly ambitious about what they can achieve by when. In the long run, this leads to disappointment and a possible self-defeating pattern where they always fail to live up to their own expectations. The perfectionist client is another version of this kind of viewpoint. Challenge this by describing what you have witnessed in the client, repeat back some phrases they have used that show their optimism or perfectionism, and then discuss how the outcomes haven't matched the expectations.

Pessimist

At the other extreme, this negative thinker has already decided that they will fail before they start out. You can challenge this in the same way as you would the optimist.

Procrastinator

The procrastinator is the client who keeps telling you they will take some action, yet always has an excuse as to why it's not happened. This is really a variation of a victim mentality. Be on the level and suggest that the action is 'off the agenda' – and ask what it needs to be replaced with.

Challenging distorted thinking

In Chapter 7 ('Listening skills'), we explored the metamodels of distortions, deletions and generalisms. These are key aspects to challenge, and the questions offered within this chapter could be useful to help you address them.

Another excellent technique to help us challenge is 'reframing' (from NLP). This is where we literally provide a different frame of reference for the client to re-examine their opinions or beliefs, encouraging them to re-evaluate them – or at least expand their viewpoint. There are a total of 14 suggested ways to reframe, known as 'sleight of mouth' techniques, devised by Robert Dilts (1990). Let's take an example belief, which sounds like it could be distorted, and one you wish to challenge: 'I know I am ugly, that's why no one loves me'. Here are some 'sleight of mouth' techniques you could use to 'reframe' this belief, each serving to dislodge the fixed, habitual belief to allow a more open and realistic perspective. Use carefully with plenty of rapport as they can sound abrasive:

- *Chunk up* – exaggerate and expand the belief to a higher, general level so that it becomes more universal and harder to believe:
  ○ 'So, do you think all ugly people are unloved?'
- *Chunk down* – get very specific about some tiny facet of the belief:
  ○ 'Your mother loves you – why is this then?'
- *Apply to self* – turn the comment back on themselves somehow:
  ○ 'Would you love an ugly person?'
- *Metaframe* – challenge the assumptions within the belief, rather than the belief itself:
  ○ 'So, by whose definition are you classifying yourself as ugly?'
- *Counterexample* – offer one piece of evidence that disproves the statement:
  ○ 'Can you think of just one person, whom you consider ugly, who is also loved?'
- *Intent* – here, you focus and comment on what you think is the intent behind the belief:
  ○ 'That sounds to me like a defence mechanism you use to avoid being loved.'
- *Change frame size* – change the scale of the belief – by size or time – make it much smaller or larger:
  ○ 'Who defines what is and isn't ugly anyway? What about the whole animal kingdom? Could that explain why some animals are extinct now?'

Dealing with negative client reactions

First, when you are challenging be aware of the client's subtle reactions to your message. They may show signs of increasing irritation through their body language, even though their verbal reaction may seem calm and rational.

It's okay to back off once you've suggested an alternative viewpoint. Some clients will think about it after the coaching session and be prepared to take it on board once they have considered it for a while. Ask the client how they feel about discussing it and accept their decision if they want to drop it. Bide your time and they may raise this themselves in the future. If not, ultimately the responsibility for change is theirs, not yours. You've done your bit by raising their awareness through your challenge.

Clients could have an emotional reaction as a result of your challenge. They may get angry, start blaming others or criticizing you, or in my experience, most often become tearful. Whatever their reaction, do not take responsibility for it. If you start feeling guilt or blame, you are hooked into the client's systemic behavioural responses. Keep an emotional distance, but accept and validate the client's right to respond in whatever way they want to. Allow them to react in whatever way they want and give them time to express their feelings. Obviously, if the situation turns nasty to the point that you feel threatened, you will need to take steps to end the session and stay safe. Tears are often positive in the long run. The client is able to let out their emotions and then can deal with the challenge in a responsible manner.

Improving your challenging skills

Improve your ability to challenge effectively as a coach by taking responsibility to speak up assertively more often in your life in general. If you tend to sit on the fence and ignore your friends' and family's negative behaviours or distorted beliefs, you are likely to find it harder to challenge a client. On the other hand, as a newly trained coach, do not make it your mission to sort out all your nearest and dearest's difficulties without their permission. They will soon tire of it. Pick your moments and challenge in a co-operative and positive way when a suitable opportunity presents itself.

Summary

- Challenging can mean giving feedback – facts (objective) or opinions (subjective).
- It can also mean helping the client see a different perspective, gained by offering a viewpoint, asking a question or suggesting an actual physical challenge.
- Be assertive when you challenge – stay on the level and use the five stages of assertive communication.
- Be aware of transactional analysis and different ego states when challenging – stay in your adult state and talk to the client as an adult.
- Time your challenge appropriately and know what kind of thing may be appropriate to challenge.
- Use questions to reframe the client's perspective when they have a negative or distorted belief.
- Be willing to change the subject if the client does not want to continue, and be prepared to deal effectively with client reactions such as anger or tears.

11

Motivating skills

You can lead a horse to water, but you can't make him drink.

(Old English proverb)

What is motivation?

First, I'd like to remind you of the common definition of the word 'motivation', which is 'the inner drive to action'. Because it is an 'inner' drive, this is something that only the client can own and create. The reality is that no one can really ever truly 'motivate' someone else to do something, we can only create the right environment for a person to motivate themselves.

This basic belief that no one can 'make' another person do anything is crucial to the success of a life coach, and also for their own sense of job satisfaction. If you base your success solely on the actions that your client manages to implement, not only will you create unnecessary anxiety for yourself, but also·your own motivation for the client to succeed could be greater than theirs. If that happens, you could find the client absolving responsibility for their actions altogether. The client's actions become your worry, not theirs. So, the best you can do for a client is to create the right environment so that they feel motivated to take whatever action is necessary to move forward.

Within the framework of a coaching session, we tend to think of the motivating part as coming right at the end, when we are helping the client develop actions as a result of the coaching conversation. In truth, we are building motivation throughout the whole session, from the very beginning. In fact, probably the most important part of building motivation comes at the beginning, when you are helping the client to get clear about their goals. I learnt many years ago a very simple framework for motivation: (a) find out what the person wants; (b) show them how to get it. People are only really ever motivated by going after what they want, not what they should have, or what their partner wants. In the 'finding out part', a person becomes far more enthusiastic about the goal when they spend time exploring it and 'trying it on for size'. In coaching, we encourage clients to 'wallow' in their goals, imagining they have already achieved them and noticing what looks, sounds and feels different. All this increases their desire to work towards their goal as now they have a crystal clear vision of exactly what they are aiming for. With coaching, we help them discover how to get it, rather than show them with our own ideas.

Theories of motivation

Behaviorism

Behaviourist B. F. Skinner developed the famous 'Pavlov's dog' experiment, which gave us the 'Stimulus–response– reward' model of behaviourism, which in turn led to the whole 'cognitive-behavioural' approach to therapy, and more recently has been adapted to coaching. Behaviourism is based on the view that most of what we do as human beings is done as a habit. Given a certain trigger, we are likely to behave in a certain way, which we have learned in the past gives us a certain reward. This forms a predictable pattern of behaviour, which no longer requires thought. With this basic premise in mind, if you can find out what triggers already motivate a client into taking a certain desired action, you can help them explore ways to generate more of these triggers in their life. You can also help them feel more motivated by having them explore the 'rewards' they may gain by taking certain actions.

This theory is also useful in understanding why people

are motivated to do destructive things, for example smoke or over-eat. By helping them identify the triggers, they may be able to avoid them. It is also very useful to explore the rewards that they get from these destructive behaviours, many of which may be beneath their conscious awareness. By bringing these out into the open, the client may discover that they no longer want these rewards or can create alternative ways to get the same kind of reward.

Motivational interviewing

A counselling approach using this basic theory was developed by Miller and Rollnick (2002) known as 'motivational interviewing'. They talk about the dilemma of change being ambivalence:

> Feeling two ways about something or someone is a common enough experience. In fact a person who feels no ambivalence about anything is hard to imagine. . . To explore ambivalence is to work at the heart of the problem of being stuck. Until a person can resolve the 'I want to, but I don't want to' dilemma, change is likely to be slow-going and short-lived.

> (2002: 13–14)

Two important questions to ask within motivational interviewing framework are:

- How important do you consider this change on a scale of 1–10?
- How confident are you to make this change?

Both these scores need to be high for a person to feel motivated. The process is directive in that you are focusing the client's attention in key areas, but remains client focused in that the impetus/reason comes from them, not you. Motivational interviewing is also about rolling with resistance but pointing out discrepancies between higher values and unwanted behaviours. The client begins to sort out their ambivalence by creating a list of benefits and costs, for both making a change (taking an action) or staying the same (doing nothing).

Logical levels

In Chapter 5 we explored Dilt's logical levels. This model is also useful for reviewing a client's lack of motivation and finding strategies to overcome it. Let's say the client says, in response to a suggested action, 'I can't do that here'. You could explore this negative belief according to which logical level it exists on. Now, it could come from any level, but listen to the word that gets emphasized as this will tell you where the stuckness is coming from:

- I can't do that *here* (the environment is the problem)
- I can't do *that* here (the behaviour is the problem)
- I can't *do* that here (the capability is the problem)
- I *can't* do that here (the beliefs/values are the problem)
- *I* can't do that here (identity is the problem).

Whichever level holds the problem, tackle solutions at the next level up. For example, if the environment is the problem, you could say: 'Okay, you don't think you could take that action in the hostile environment you have described. So let's look at the behaviours you can control that could positively affect that environment. What could you do that would help move this forward?'

'Chunking up' and 'towards/away from' motives

One excellent technique for checking this out is to use the NLP technique of 'chunking up' for higher-level values. When the client says what they want to achieve, you ask 'What will that give you?'. You can then ask the same question of whatever they answer next. Are you left with a pure, strong positive value like 'I can be truly happy' or does it end up being a 'fix' to a negative: 'She'll finally stop nagging me'?

Within NLP, there are two kinds of approaches to motivation: 'towards' and 'away from' – already mentioned in Chapter 2. People tend to favour one or other of these approaches. 'Away from' people are motivated to get away from the problem, out of the danger zone, to put the fire out, etc. They are more motivated to get away from a problem than to move towards a solution. This kind of person may start off really motivated in coaching sessions when they really feel 'close' to the problem. As they start to become more successful, their initial drive may wane.

You see people with this kind of motivation who fail to lose weight. They start their new diet when the scales tip to a certain weight that they perceive as a problem. For a few weeks they are zealous about losing the weight and hugely motivated to stick with the diet. However, once they lose a few pounds, the initial enthusiasm wears off as they are no longer so close to the problem. They start to cheat a little and find themselves slowly slipping back. . .

Examples of 'towards' and 'away from' language are as follows:

- 'I just want to get out of sales altogether. I'm fed up with being micro-managed and the car is rubbish.' *(This is 'away from' language.)*
- 'I want to be happier in my life. I've had all sorts of difficulties to overcome over the last few years, but now I just want to move on and start living the life I always wanted.' *(This is 'towards' language.)*
- 'I want to lose that extra stone I've been carrying around for the last five years. I want to wear the kind of clothes I used to wear.' *(This is a bit of a mixture of 'towards' and 'away from' language.)*

'Towards' people are motivated to get somewhere. Generally with this kind of motivation the client is more likely to stick with actions and get results. You can help a client see what they might want to move towards with the question 'What will that give you?'.

The stages of change model

A useful model to bear in mind when considering your client's attitude to change is Prochaska and DiClemente's (1983) 'stages of change model' developed in the late 1970s and early 1980s through studies of smokers who were successful in quitting. In this model, there are six stages of change, and the client's perception of change and attitude towards it will be different at each stage. How long each stage takes will vary tremendously from client to client. The client decides when they are ready to move to the next stage, not you as their coach. The underlying wisdom in this model is that the only effective and sustainable change is that which occurs as a result of the client's decision to change, not by pressure from others. The following represents my interpretation of the change model.

Stage 1: Pre-contemplation

At this stage, the person has no knowledge or recognition that change is required. They are blissfully unaware that their own behaviour is causing problems. They seem to have 'blind spots' or 'blinkers' that help them avoid acknowledging how their own problem behaviour may be impacting on their lives.

You may be coaching them on some other aspect of their life, and see hints and clues that a certain behaviour is a problem and change is required. However, if they don't see it there is little you can do. If relevant and appropriate, you could ask a question or two in connection with this topic and sow the seed. BUT, remember that the choice is theirs and they will not change if they are not ready to. Let them know that you completely accept their perception and don't put any pressure on them to see things differently.

Stage 2: Contemplation

At this stage, the client is considering the possibility of change. They may acknowledge that their behaviour needs addressing. They may be arguing with themselves about the merits of change versus the status quo. The change they anticipate is some way off in the distance. They are not ready to take action on it just yet, although they are open to more information to help them think about it. Some people remain at this stage forever, never moving forwards to the next stage.

Again, it is important not to exert pressure on the client. You could suggest that they draw up a list of pros and cons to the change, for instance. Encourage them to become more aware of what's going on around them in connection to the change. Help them investigate ways to gain more information to help them decide what to do next. Help them think about all the potential benefits to change – which may start by identifying new goals to work towards in connection with this change.

Stage 3: Preparation

Here the client is ready to 'test out' making the change. The change seems possible now and the motivation to make it is increasing. They are gathering information, resources and support to help them make the change. They can see the change happening in the near future. They are saying things like 'I've got to do this' and 'I know I can change'. This is an important stage as it builds determination.

Here all your coaching skills and techniques will be valuable. Help the client set achievable goals and measures for success. Identify potential blocks or issues and help the client find ways around these. And, of course, agree action points.

Stage 4: Action

Here the change is happening. The client is demonstrating and practising the new behaviours required. They are consciously using their willpower to keep the changed behaviour. The client could stay in this stage for three to six months after change has occurred.

Help the client by acknowledging their success and keep reminding them of the benefits. Help them identify support networks. Discuss short-term rewards they can give themselves and help them see their behaviour change in a way that boosts their self-confidence. Help them deal with any negative feelings or longings to go back to the way they were.

Stage 5: Maintenance

This is the stage six months to five years after the change. The client continues to be committed to the change. Occasional 'slips' are noticed and dealt with, as the person is able to resist temptation. The change is gradually integrated into their life and new behaviours become habits.

Stage 6: Relapse

This is the possible stage that occurs when the client has 'forgotten' that the behaviour was ever a problem, and slips back to the old way, barely noticing it has occurred. The client may feel very discouraged. Help the client recognize the 'trigger' back to the old behaviour and discuss ways to deal with it in the future. Help the client accept that relapse is very common and doesn't mean that ultimate success is not possible. Encourage them to try again.

A possible seventh stage: Transcendence

Eventually, if successful in the maintenance stage for long enough, the person can avoid relapse and move to this final stage when the change is fully integrated and the old behaviour would seem alien and peculiar. It is unlikely that your services as a coach are required here! However, if a client is seeking to make a change in another aspect of their life, it would be worth exploring if they have successfully made any change before and reached this stage. You could explore with them how they handled each stage of change, and use this information to help plan how best to manage the new change.

Think about someone who is a smoker, for instance. They come to you, as a life coach, to focus on their health. When you ask about their smoking they say 'No, it doesn't affect my health at all. My father smokes too and is fighting fit at 93 years old!'. They are in 'pre-contemplation' with regard the potential change of 'giving up smoking'. If you, as a coach, decide you know best and start to drop hints or overly focus on this area, you are in danger of alienating your client. More importantly, the client is likely to become more entrenched in their own views that no change is required, as they combat your suggestions otherwise. Far better to wait for glimmers of the client's own recognition, showing that they are moving into the second stage of change – contemplation. They may flit in and out of this stage, so catch them at the moment they seem to become aware of the need for change and the possibility it could happen. Support and build on their own awareness, rather than push them to take action.

Creating a compelling vision

Vague goals seldom motivate. The more unclear a goal is, the harder it is to know what to do to achieve it. With no clear way forward, energy levels will be low around actually making any effort. As covered earlier in this book, most of the first session with a client is likely to focus purely on getting really clear on goals. A further technique to build motivation from the start of a session is to get the client to really connect to what it would be like if they were to achieve their goal. Ask the client to imagine that they have achieved their goal. What does it feel like? What's different about themselves and the world around them? Get them to visualize this and describe all they can see, hear and feel in this imaginary future.

By exploring and 'twiddling' with the aspects of the sounds, sensations and pictures, you can help a client raise the intensity of their desire to achieve change. For example, their imagined 'picture' of success within their mind's eye might be a small, black-and-white still image, which is a bit out of focus and doesn't have much detail. Given time you can encourage the client to try 'seeing' the same picture in colour, much larger and possibly as a moving image rather than a still 'photograph'. When they picture themselves having achieved something, can they see themselves in the picture, or are they imagining this as though 'looking through their own eyes'? For most, the feelings are more intense when they are inside the picture, looking out.

With the sounds, can they hear their own voice talking about their success? If not, what happens if they imagine that too? What other sounds can they imagine accompanying this image of success? How about an inspirational, uplifting piece of music? Get them to experiment with the 'soundtrack' and see which one works. Get them to connect with the feelings and sensations this success creates in them. This could be a warm glow in their heart, or a buzz of energy around their whole body etc.

Once a client is really fired up by what the achievement would mean to them, finish by getting them to picture themselves disassociated (i.e. looking at a picture of themselves from an external perspective, rather than as if through their own eyes). In this way, the unconscious mind will strive towards getting back to it.

To take this idea a step further, another excellent way to build motivation is to use clean language (see Chapter 8: 'Questioning skills') to develop a metaphor for their ultimate goal. For example, if you ask 'And when you can finally be happy, that's like what?', they may reply 'It's like I'm a bird soaring up high in the sky, free and flexible'. Then have them connect to the metaphor by really exploring the details of it. For example you could ask:

- 'What kind of bird is that bird?'
- 'Is there anything else about soaring?'

Identifying and resolving inner conflict

When a client says something along the lines of 'Part of me wants to do this, part of me doesn't', you know there is some kind of inner conflict that may prevent them moving forwards with their goal. You can explore the different parts by using a *'parts integration'* exercise. In this NLP process you can help the client actually visualize the two parts within themselves that have a difference of opinion. This is a relatively straightforward exercise that lends itself to many adaptions. A simple version is to ask the client to imagine one part of themselves in one hand, and the other in the other hand. The client can begin to integrate the parts through exploring the differences and similarities between these parts, and also by physically slowly bringing their hands together and noticing how they feel/what comes up for them.

You could use clean language to develop the metaphoric parts, then ask each part (rather than asking the question of the client themselves) what they want. You can then start a dialogue of negotiation between the two parts, verbalized by the client. What can both these parts agree on? What higher purpose are they both seeking to achieve?

Another variation of an NLP exercise I use when I suspect an inner conflict is the 'Who are you' exercise. I simply ask the client this simple question around nine or ten times, each time having them describe their answer in detail, before representing that part of themselves on a yellow sticky that they then place somewhere in the room around them, before I ask 'And who else are you?' In this way, the client can see all aspects of the different sides of themselves and how any conflict may be preventing them from taking action. Again, some negotiations can take place and also some rebalancing of the 'power' distributed among the internal parts of themselves.

Agreeing action points

Action points should always be those actions suggested and agreed by the client. These are the things that they will feel most motivated to achieve. You may have an idea for an action (usually presented as an 'assignment') in which case be careful to ensure that the client takes ownership of it, and you don't just add it in by telling them to do this one as well. Chances are it won't happen! Introduce an assignment by first letting your client know that you have an idea for an assignment that will help them achieve goal x, and then asking them whether they would be interested in hearing about it. If they say yes, explain it to the client then ask them if they would like to add this to their agreed actions. You can also ask if they would like it to replace one of their own actions or have it as an additional one. The assignment could be presented as a 'challenge', as mentioned in the previous chapter.

I usually suggest to a client that they identify three key actions to take in-between sessions, although this is not a hard-and-fast rule. I learn quickly the clients who like a list of actions and those who work best with a single, key action to focus all their attention on.

How do you get from exploring possibilities to agreeing

actions, within a coaching conversation? With the clean language approach we would ask:

- 'What needs to happen for . . . [whatever their clarified, all-singing, all-dancing goal has become . . .]?'
- 'And is there anything else that needs to happen for. . .?'

With this approach, occasionally clients will wriggle out of the responsibility and give 'conditions' that they cannot control themselves, such as:

- 'I need to win the lottery.'
- 'My wife needs to change first.'

To take a condition for change and turn it into an action requires a further question, which begins with 'Can. . .?':

- 'Can you win the lottery?'
- 'Can your wife change?'

This helps a client see they have no control over the condition, but may be able to influence it. So you could ask:

- 'What needs to happen for your wife to change?'
- 'Could you explain to her exactly how you feel about her behaviour?'

This now sounds like a solid, do-able action step that is within the client's control. You may need to check a bit further:

- 'And can you explain that to her?'

If they say yes with some confidence, you have a commitment to an action.

When you have the appropriate number of actions agreed, it is worthwhile to quantify them still further until they become real and tangible to the client:

- 'So when will you explain that to her?'
- 'How long will it take?'
- 'Can you pencil that time in your diary right now?'
- 'What do you need to do before then in order to be prepared for that conversation?'

Getting a rating for commitment and raising the level

You also need to check how committed the client is taking each action. You could do this by asking the following questions:

- 'What could prevent you from taking that action?'
- 'How can you tackle these obstacles should they come along?'
- 'On a scale of 1–10, how committed are you right now in talking this action?'

This scaling question is really useful to gauge just how motivated and committed the client is in taking the agreed action. If the score is lower than seven or eight, you could help the client explore this further by asking the following questions:

- 'What needs to happen for you to increase that score by one point? And another point?'
- 'What needs to happen for you to feel totally committed to taking this action?'

Sometimes these questions alone help the client adjust their desire so that commitment soars to a nine or ten. As well as getting a verbal confirmation of a client's commitment, you can notice shifts in energy as an indication of the inner drive or 'spark' coming alive in the client. As a client's motivation increases, they are likely to sit up straighter and become more animated. You may feel the energy increasing within you too as you unconsciously pick up on this energy. However, for the client who is lacking motivation, they are likely to be remain still and show little movement. This is a clue that you need to explore things further with the client so that they feel more motivated to take action.

The attributes of a great motivator

Good motivators help people to believe in themselves. Your belief in your client's ability to succeed will affect their own confidence. Simply verbalizing 'I believe that you can do this' will help increase the client's confidence. Good motivators can transfer their enthusiasm to others by having high levels of energy that they effectively communicate through their words, voice and body language. There is a certain 'buzz' or animation that transmits from them. Finally, good motivators have a conviction of success. You can show the client how much faith you have by talking about the achievement of certain actions as a foregone conclusion, rather than a doubtful one. For example, you could say 'Next time we can explore xxx as you will have done xxx by then', rather than 'Depending how you get on with your actions we might be able to. . .'.

Summary

- You can't make someone want to do something; concentrate on creating the right environment so that they decide for themselves.
- Nearly all behaviour is learned – from previous stimuli/rewards we get stuck in a pattern.
- One key to increasing motivation is to remove ambivalence.
- Another is to chunk up to a higher purpose or value, which becomes a more compelling vision.
- Resolve internal conflict by getting the client to start a dialogue between conflicting parts.
- As you approach the end of a coaching session, begin to explore possible actions that have arisen in the client's mind during the session.
- Gauge the level of energy and commitment the client feels about taking a certain action. Ask them what would need to happen for that energy and commitment to increase.
- Be specific: 'What will you do and how will you do that? When will it happen? Can you write that in your diary right now?'

12

Marketing skills

Very few coaches I meet seem confident about their marketing skills. For many coaches, the idea of encouraging people to buy from them is somehow untasteful. Many think of marketing as a necessary evil, but one that remains a 'dark art' that they would rather remain ignorant about.

Having come from a sales and marketing background, I personally enjoy marketing and see it as an integral part of coaching. After all, how can you help someone to achieve their life goals without first helping them make the decision to do something positive about it, i.e. commit to a series of coaching sessions by you?

Myths of marketing

The following are some of the common myths I often hear from coaches when talking about marketing.

Myth 1: Marketing is something I need to find extra time for in addition to running my business

Marketing *is* running your business. When you are coaching, you are being your product. Virtually everything else you do is marketing. If you are at capacity regarding your coaching practice, with an abundance of ideal clients, then you still need to devote time to ensure you keep the momentum going. If it is not true, then when you are not coaching, what are you doing that's more important than marketing? Whatever it is, reprioritize if you want your business to succeed. The ideal ratio of coaching activity to marketing is about 80: 20, i.e. 80 per cent doing the job, 20 per cent marketing to get the work. That's about one day a week devoted to marketing activity, or an hour or so every day. For a new business, it is likely to be considerably more until your business becomes established: probably 80 per cent or more of your time will be spent on marketing.

Myth 2: Marketing is too difficult for me to do well

The beauty of marketing is that there are many different ways to achieve the same thing. Some marketing techniques you will enjoy more than others, some you will find easier. You can choose which aspects of marketing you wish to devote regular time to, and as long as you cover all the bases, you will reap the rewards.

Myth 3: I'll get all the business through word of mouth

There are some businesses that manage to survive in this way, with an excellent product and a great deal of luck, or they've built up to this position after years of hard work. You can effectively market yourself to encourage the 'word-of-mouth' referral process. However, it is unrealistic to believe that it is a reliable way to guarantee a steady flow of clients, especially if you are a relatively new business in a new and competitive industry such as coaching.

Myth 4: Marketing is expensive

Certainly, some haphazard marketing activities can cost a lot more than they reap. For instance, unfocused advertising without any strategy can eat up your entire marketing budget very quickly. Some marketing can be high cost and high gain – if you have the budget and the bottle to do it. Some marketing is reasonably priced, and some is completely free – except for your own time investment. Sometimes paying for it can be more cost-effective in terms of your time outlay. Overall, it's fair to say that you can find marketing activities to suit every budget.

***Myth 5: Marketing is forcing people to buy. I don't like
being pushy. I'm too nice for that. I'll wait for people
to come to me***

This is the most common fallacy of all, borne from a mindset
of fear. That is, the fear of rejection. You don't want to annoy
people, so you are just too nice to sell yourself, too modest to
'blow your own trumpet'. Selling is one of the steps within
the marketing process and all businesses need to sell products to customers. Some do it through advertising, some
through formal presentations. Many businesses nowadays do
it through websites and other internet mechanisms. Without
selling, the rest of the marketing function becomes a bit
pointless. Selling is the interaction between you and your
customer that persuades them to buy you and your product
now.

When I've asked coaches for the real reasons why they
don't do more to promote their business, they tell me it's
because they don't like selling, which they see as 'forcing'
people to buy from them. The underlying emotion is fear, and
it's the irrational fear of rejection. If we don't actually make
an offer to someone, then no one need reject us. Of course,
we don't get any business, but at least we don't feel snubbed.
How selfish of you! If you truly believe in your product and
feel that coaching can help people make real positive changes
in their life, how cruel not to tell them! By explaining what
you do to the right kind of people and giving them a good
reason to buy from you, you are providing each person with a
choice. Good coaching is all about helping people have more
choices. The person can always say no. You don't have to
take it personally. And, more likely if a person doesn't say
yes, they may say 'maybe, please keep in touch'. This is one
step nearer to them buying from you, no pressure exerted.
Everyone is happy, including you.

Some coaches feel that coaching and selling are opposite ends of a spectrum. As a coach, you help people solve
problems in a non-directive, empathic way. You just don't
see yourself as a hardnosed salesperson. Who says that all
salespeople are hardnosed? If that is your view, then you
have a negative stereotypical view of salespeople. I came

from a sales background, and good salespeople are taught questioning and listening techniques that are, guess what, very similar to coaching! A good salesperson is going through a very similar process to that of a coach. That is, asking the client questions to help them discover for themselves the right solution.

Exercise: Changing your beliefs about marketing

If you could choose five of the most positive, empowering and motivating beliefs you can about marketing your business, what would these five beliefs be?

1

2

3

4

5

Now, for each belief, rate how much you actually buy into this belief right now, out of 10. Be honest with yourself! Then, against each belief, write down what evidence you would need to confirm and strengthen this belief. And then: what you can do to start collecting this evidence.

Key marketing skills to work on

Detailed below are the key marketing skills you need to develop and then continually improve on, in order to effectively market a coaching business.

Skill 1: Ability to develop a clear niche

Let's start with definitions. The word 'niche' has many meanings, and I am using the word in a business sense, which I define as: a narrowly defined group of potential customers for you to focus and target your marketing effects towards. It also has a number of other definitions:

- a situation or activity best suited to a person's interests, ability or nature;

- a special area of demand for a product or service;
- a crevice or foothold in a rock or wall (what an interesting definition: a place where you, and only, you can fit – and climb up as you develop and grow);
- (and from the world of ecology) the function or position of an organism within an ecological community.

I like the last definition. Your niche is the area for you to specialize in that is right for you and your environment, given your life experience, current situation, abilities and expertise.

The word itself comes from the French word *nichier*, which means 'to nest'. Also an old Italian word *nicchio*, which means 'seashell'. Both of these images conjure up for me a sense of the 'naturalness' of niche marketing, and how important it is not just for business success, but also for life happiness.

All in all, it's more than just a target market. It is the best fit for you, given who you are and where you are in your life: a natural and comfortable place from which you can grow.

Example niche markets
A niche market is a group of people with at least two things in common, for example:

- same problem/need;
- same type of person/interests/situation.

So, it could be:

- women returning to work after children and needing a confidence boost;
- newly divorced men who want to start dating again and don't know how;
- small business owners who don't have time to grow their business through marketing.

In all these examples, the type of person and their specific problem is clear and distinct.

Another example of a niche market that I've heard recently is people who have lost their way and are seeking a new direction. However, this is not a niche market. It could apply to virtually anyone as we have no detail on what type of 'lost' they need to be and which new direction they may be seeking. It is too vague, and there is the danger that it will appeal to no one. Now you may use words like these in your marketing material, however first and foremost you would have already clearly identified the type of problem and the key audience for your message.

For a niche market to work well for you, the people within it need to have a few more vital ingredients:

- Would they believe you have the experience and capability to help them with their problem/need?
- Do you believe you have the experience and capability to help them with their problem/need?
- Can they afford to pay you?
- Will they see themselves as you do? How would they describe themselves and is it the same description as you have for them?
- Can you identify and reach them at a suitable time (when they recognize they have a need and are willing to buy)?
- Do they congregate somewhere online and/or in a real location where you can deliver your niche marketing message to them?
- Are there enough of them out there for you to establish a viable customer base?
- Is your niche group small enough to be a unique market and one that you can specialize in servicing?

Why niche?

It is easy to get enthusiastic about your products and services and believe that they could help anyone ... achieve many different things. You may be right, however that's a difficult marketing message to get out. Where do you start? And when you are marketing to everyone, everyone is just a bunch of 'someones', and each someone will have their own unique situation, need or problem they want addressed. The more you can talk and write about that specific need in your marketing material, the more you will attract the right kind of person.

Sometimes the fear of not generating enough work means

we want to spread the net as far and as wide as possible to catch any type of client. Using that particular metaphor, the wider the net, the weaker it becomes, so rather than catch more, you may in fact catch nothing. The more general the message, the more diluted it becomes. The most extreme example of this would be to see a nice big advert that says 'I can help anyone to do anything'. This becomes an empty and unbelievable statement.

When you have defined a niche for your marketing efforts, you will:

- make more effective use of resources and effort: you'll save time with a consistent message, continually building your reputation and credibility to the same group, rather than starting from scratch every few weeks;
- find it easier to market/sell: it is so much easier to write a marketing message when you can be specific about the results you bring, and can use case studies, examples and analogues to bring your message alive. A niched marketing message sounds more believable and convincing so you are going to get better results;
- get remembered/get referrals: the narrower and more specific your niche is, the better it will be remembered. You will be remembered and people will refer others to you, especially if you are the only person they know in this particular area/niche;
- get to work with the kind of people who energize and inspire you to be your best, which means you will find it easier to say 'no' when appropriate, without feeling guilty;
- have the opportunity to change your mind about your niche in the future. Most people will. As we change and evolve as people, the service and expertise we want to offer is also likely to change.

How to go about choosing a niche

What do you sell?
Not the raw material, the end result. What do you do for someone? What will they gain? What will they become when they buy from you? The techniques you use are not what you

sell. They are your tools, and if they are good, you'll do a better job. But that's not what people are buying.

Think of people you have helped in the past. What solutions or results did they gain from working with you? Think of the ideal customer you feel drawn to help. What problems do they have? What do they need and want to achieve? What kind of result or solution can you imagine they will get from your coaching?

Who do you sell to?

What type of person best benefits from what you sell? What types of problems do they have? Who has bought from you in the past? What similarities or characteristics can you identify? What type of person are you finding yourself helping at the moment?

Be specific on their identity – sex, age, stage of life, job role, family circumstances, location, lifestyle, income bracket, dreams, goals, fears, etc. Think about what they may be doing at the moment to address their problem – joining associations, reading newsletters/magazines, searching the internet, getting makeovers, investing, etc. Think about what else they may be doing in their lives, e.g. hobbies, leisure activities, how they travel, etc. The clearer picture you have of this ideal person, the easier you will find it to communicate your marketing message and to find ways to reach them with it.

Tips for discovering your niche

Discovering your niche can be an elusive process. Sometimes we fail to notice the 'blindingly obvious' signals and signs all around us that signpost our way forward. Sometimes we are in conflict. A part of us wants to go one way, another part has a different idea. Some people are so full of great ideas and possibilities that they find it very difficult to whittle this down to just one group of people with a certain set of requirements. Most people find that the best niche group for them is a group of people who are already known to them, people they understand and relate to, people who will view them with some credibility. A word of advice – be sure to choose a niche group of people you really like being with, or you will soon hate your job!

If you can discover a group of people that you feel passionate and positive about helping, and truly energized by coaching them, you'll find it much, much easier to market to them. If you are still uncertain as to your ideal niche, you may want to consider working one-on-one with a coach to explore your strengths, values and goals.

Warning! Choosing the wrong kind of niche
What factors led to you choosing a career in coaching? Why you? Why now? Scratch a little beneath the surface, and I suggest that the answer in many cases could be more selfish than we are willing to admit initially. Many coaches discover that the person they feel most compelled to work with is the one with the same issues and goals as they themselves have. Unfortunately, you may not be the right person for these types of people, as you are too close to their issues and your ability to be impartial and non-judgemental could be affected. So, you need to ask yourself:

- What similarities do you have with your target group?
- How might this connection affect your ability to work with this group?

A useful way to discover a group that you are motivated to help but also could be impartial towards is to answer the following question:

- Who were you before you were who you are today?

This question gets you to explore previous issues and goals that were once a big part of who you were, but not anymore. The chances are, these are things you have successful dealt with in your life. Could you effectively coach people currently dealing with these issues and goals? Your experience means you will quickly gain credibility in this area.

Skill 2: Ability to explain your niche message clearly and persuasively – verbally and in writing

In its simplest form, you need to be able to sum up your product in one succinct sentence: '*I help [a certain kind of person] to [overcome a certain kind of problem] so they get [a certain kind of solution]*. From this basic starting point, you can develop the right words to explain this verbally or to present it in writing on a website, business card, leaflet or any other sales materials. Your purpose in explaining your niche message is twofold:

1 to let people know you exist;
2 to give them a good reason to keep in touch.

A clear niche statement along the lines given above may satisfy both these purposes. The extra information you obviously need to give is all your contact details. To add an extra incentive to keep in touch, for your written messages you could add in a line that offers a free report, taster session or other 'gift' that will be of relative value to your ideal client. The best kind of give-aways are those with 'How to' titles, focused on a specific aspect of your ideal client's likely information requirements. In this way, your give-away serves two purposes – it will be useful for the client, plus by the very fact they want this information, you know they have the kind of needs that your coaching will be able to satisfy.

In Chapter 6 we explored relationship building and networking. Having these simple messages in place is enough to start this process. Use your niche statement, contact details and free offer as the basic construction of your business card, your email signature, basic advertisements and any other small medium you can use to get your message out there.

You will also want to expand on this basic message for other media, such as leaflets and websites. Put yourself in your customers' shoes and imagine what they might want to know over and above the very basic message you have already communicated. I suggest you follow this basic structure:

- *Relate to the reader*, by describing 'typical' clients and the problems they have. Describe aspects of the kind of person they may be. Use 'you' in your language, and ask rhetorical questions that you expect your ideal client would say 'yes' to.
- *Questions and answers*: now imagine the kinds of questions the reader may have about the service you offer. List the

questions and provide simple, straightforward answers. Tell them how it works, what they can expect and what is likely to happen as a result. Give examples and analogues to help make the points.

- *Why you?* Explain your credentials, offer the facts and the benefit each fact brings – try adding 'which means that' to the end of each point you make. Give them some background about you and your story so far.
- *Convince them that it works*: expect the reader to be skeptical, and offer quotes from satisfied customers. You can also offer any added-value quality benefits, such as any professional association's code of ethics you abide by, or money-back guarantees.
- Finally, and most importantly, *tell them what to do next*. Remind them of your free offer and also explain how they may take the first step towards coaching with you. If you haven't done so already, give them an idea of the cost, and any package price.

Altogether, this information can form the basis of a simple website. You may get someone else to design this for you, but by sorting out the written message for each of the above categories you will make the website designer's job much easier. You can also use this structure to explain verbally what you do. In a one-to-one conversation, this can become more two way, with actual questions asked along the way, as well as explaining more about what you do. How do you find the most effective ways to describe your services? An interesting way to explore this and get ideas is to imagine yourself as your client.

Exercise: Put yourself in your client's shoes
This exercise is based on an NLP technique known as 'second positioning'. Focus on an empty chair, and imagine that your ideal client is sitting in it right now. What do they look like? What are they wearing? What are they talking about? Where have they come from and where are they going? When you have a really strong visualization going, get up and sit in that chair yourself, and imagine that as you do, you take on the persona of your ideal client. As the client, what would

you like to happen? What questions do you have? What concerns do you have? What do you need answered? Where will you go for the answers? Jot down your questions. Take these questions and use them to search the internet. This should lead you to competitors who are offering similar services to you, as well as other sources of information relevant to your niche market.

Skill 3: Ability to communicate your niche message regularly and consistently through focused channels of communication

Persistence is a vital element to successful marketing, as Hannah McNamara (2007) explains in her excellent book *Niche Marketing for Coaches*: 'Many coaches run one or two adverts, send out a sales letter, make a few phone calls and wonder why they aren't drowning in clients. The reality is that you need to be consistently marketing yourself' (2007: 172). Your focused channels of communication include two elements: *what* media you use to communicate, and *where* you communicate to.

In deciding the media, it's good to have a range of options, but bear in mind your strengths and preferences. Some coaches find article-writing an excellent way of getting their niche message out there. Some like to attend events and network, others are happy to deliver stand-up presentations. Find the one key media that suits you and really go to town on it. Paid-for advertising is another medium you can use, but to be effective you need to commit to it long term, and to be really effective it needs to be placed somewhere where many of your ideal clients will see it, e.g. in a specialist magazine.

So where else can you deliver your niche message? There are many places out there, on and offline. For example, online forums, social clubs, associations, church groups, hairdressing salons, airports, doctors' surgeries, gyms, school, libraries, etc. The key is to find places where your likely clients are likely to congregate.

The media used to initiate contact could simply be leaving a supply of business cards or leaflets for people to notice and pick up. On the other hand, with a bit of imagination, you can create opportunities for greater interaction, so your potential clients are more likely to remember you, and you can personally invite them to keep in touch. For instance, you could organize an event or workshop, run a competition, or give out a questionnaire, offering feedback to those who contact you direct with the results. You could offer free or low-cost taster sessions, or interactive telesessions in small groups.

Remember, you goal here is to connect and leave the door open for future contact, not to sell. On the other hand, from these activities you are likely to create a strong bond with a few people immediately for whom the time is right to commence coaching.

Skill 4: Ability to keep in touch with potential clients and people who will influence your potential clients

To begin with, this means cultivating your contact database – keeping it up to date, accurate and continually adding more information as you get it. Your contact database will become one of your most important assets as a coach. The larger your contact database, the bigger your client base – if you use it effectively. The key is to have a follow-up method that's useful for the potential client and reminds them that you exist and what you can do for them. It also effectively builds a relationship, as covered in the next chapter.

The easiest way to do this with large numbers of people is through some form of regular e-newsletter. This does not have to be lengthy, but needs to include some useful snippets of information relevant to your ideal clients. Other ways to keep in touch may be Christmas and birthday cards, or post-cards of special offers or 'news'. With a focused niche group you can also keep in touch through your other marketing activities, such as events, adverts and articles. Each time a potential client learns more about you, the relationship deepens, as we will see in the next chapter, and the chance of them choosing you for life coaching increases.

Finally, when a person decides to take on a life coach, they generally want to sort it out almost immediately. So when they email or call, be sure to get back to them quickly and be ready with your diary.

Summary

- In general, coaches seem to be uncomfortable with the marketing process, particularly selling, and many myths exist that help them to avoid it.
- Selling is very similar to coaching: cultivate some positive beliefs about the process and recognise the similarities in skill-set.
- Developing a clear niche – so you can succinctly say what you do and specifically who for – is the key to successful marketing.
- Create a simple marketing message that you can use consistently and regularly through a variety of different media.
- Choose marketing media that suit your strengths and preferences.
- Find the right channels to communicate your message in the right places where your ideal clients are likely to congregate.
- Build a database of contacts and have effective follow-up processes to keep in touch with them.

13

Understanding the difference between coaching and therapy

Reasons for clarity

First, let's discuss why it is so important to be clear on the difference between coaching and therapy. Many people discover that the process of coaching can work amazingly well for them in terms of making progress in their lives; allowing them to deal with and solve all sorts of issues and behavioural problems they may have had. Why, then, do we have to make a distinction and draw a very clear line between what a life coach can offer compared to a psychotherapist, or a counsellor for that matter? They are all about helping someone through talking. Surely the client doesn't care what it's called as long as it works?

Let me give you a few good reasons:

- From the *client's perspective*: you need to be very clear on the service you provide and to set expectations, so that you don't end up with an unhappy client who expected you to 'fix' them.
- From a *legal perspective*: the word 'therapy' means you are providing a 'remedial' service and as such you would need to be regulated accordingly.
- From a *moral perspective*: if you muddy the waters between the two, you will not be working ethically. Would you let your dentist operate on your appendix? Always stick with your specialism.
- From a *professional perspective*: you need to represent a clear view to the market that shows what coaching is and

how it works – for the good of the coaching industry as a whole.

- From a *personal perspective*: if you get 'out of your depth' with a client's issues, this can leave you with your own issues to resolve, such as guilt, inadequacy, regret, etc.

Definitions of psychotherapy and counselling

Both psychotherapy and counselling are forms of therapy, and start with the premise that the client or 'patient' has a problem or crisis to be 'fixed' or resolved.

Psychotherapy has been established much longer than life coaching. Early psychotherapists, such as Freud and Jung, first explored the mind and developed models to explain how people think. These models have evolved into a science, which continues to adapt and grow. The UK Council for Psychotherapy (2008: unpaginated) gives the following definition of psychotherapy:

> Psychotherapy is the provision, by a qualified practitioner, of a formal and professional relationship within which patients/clients can profitably explore difficult, and often painful, emotions and experiences. These may include feelings of anxiety, depression, trauma, or perhaps the loss of meaning of one's life. It is a process that seeks to help the person gain an increased capacity for choice, through which the individual becomes more autonomous and self-determined.

With a strong grounding in theory, psychotherapy is recognized as a legitimate profession and requires extensive training (four years postgraduate) as well as having regulations and ethics to protect both the client and the therapist.

Counselling, on the other hand, has evolved in recent years but is also seen as an orthodox approach to mental health issues. The British Association of Counselling and Psychotherapy (BACP, 2008) offers the following definition of counselling:

> Counselling takes place when a counsellor sees a client in a private and confidential setting to explore a difficulty

the client is having, distress they may be experiencing or perhaps their dissatisfaction with life, or loss of a sense of direction and purpose. It is always at the request of the client as no one can properly be 'sent' for counselling.

The BACP also explains in its factsheets that the distinction between psychotherapy and counselling is not clear-cut: it will depend on the context within which the practitioner operates and their own level of training and experience. It goes on to say: 'There are well founded traditions which use the terms interchangeably and others which distinguish between them'. The overlap between the two professions is acknowledged and accepted although, generally speaking, a psychotherapist is more likely to deal with people with more extreme mental health issues and psychological disorders than a counsellor. Another factor that connects psychotherapy and counselling is that both are available on the National Health Service (NHS). Again, this confirms that these approaches are considered for those with an 'illness' of sorts.

The differences and similarities between coaching and therapy

As we have already covered, life coaching is a service aimed at helping an individual to make progress towards their personal goals. It is normally non-directive and relies on the client's self-motivation and ability to change in order for progress to be made. The main difference with life coaching is that it is offered as a service to help a person achieve goals, with the assumption that they are a 'normal' person without mental health issues. However, the danger lies in the fact that it is not always obvious at the outset whether a client has deeper-rooted issues that may require a psychotherapeutic or counselling approach.

If you are entering the life coaching business having already trained in psychotherapy or counselling, you will already have many skills and models to help you deal effectively with coaching clients. Your aim as a coach will, however, be more forward focused and goal oriented.

Alternatively, if you are coming into life coaching with no psychotherapy or counselling skills, you will need to maintain an awareness of the scope of life coaching and its potential boundaries. It is important for you to acknowledge when it is in the client's best interests to refer them to a more specialized professional. Unfortunately, the boundaries are not always clear and, as a life coach, you will need to set your own clear parameters on when you will take on a client and when you will refer them. An added difficulty arises because clients themselves are seldom clear on the difference in approach. Some may have been to a psychotherapist or counsellor previously and expect you to follow a similar process. Many clients may just want you to listen as they recount the complex difficulties they are facing. A life coach does, however, have a responsibility to help the client navigate away from their present difficulties by focusing on their future and possible solutions, as highlighted by Jenny Rogers (2004: 15):

> Not all, but much psychotherapy looks to the past to explain the present, and the therapist is interested in answering the question 'Why?' Insight into cause and effect and the origins of emotions is a strong feature of some (though not all) schools of therapy. The coach may look briefly to the past but is more interested in the client's present and future and is probably more concerned with the question 'What?', as in 'What to do?' than in the question 'Why?'.

There are many different forms of psychotherapy, some using techniques quite similar to those used by a life coach. Unlike a life coach, a psychotherapist is likely to dig deeper into the client's psyche, exploring childhood experiences and family relationships and dynamics. Understandably, the process may take longer than counselling or life coaching. Some models for psychotherapy have been adapted to be used in counselling and life coaching.

It is important to recognize that all three disciplines draw on the same theories and models and may even use similar techniques. Although life coaching is not therapy, it is fair to say that the process of coaching often has a therapeutic benefit for the client. The crucial difference, in my opinion, lies in two key factors:

1 What is your overall intent and where is your attention drawn to?
   a A coach's intent will be on establishing the client's goals and exploring ways for them to move towards them. Attention is on the solution, although some exploration of problems/obstacles may be necessary to overcome or unblock them.
   b A counsellor's intent will be on helping the client to open up and express bottled-up feelings and emotions. Attention is on the problem, although some counsellors will also help a client move forwards.
   c A psychotherapist's intent will be on healing a patient with 'abnormal' mental issues. Their attention is also on the problem, although many psychotherapists can and do provide 'solution-based' therapy.
2 Where is the client's attention and are they able to make progress?
   a Clients who can form a clear goal and are able to articulate what they want are very likely to benefit from coaching.
   b Clients who cannot focus on the future but instead are consistently drawn to the past and to reliving the same experiences over and over, would benefit from counselling.
   c Clients who have a mental health issue so overwhelming that it affects their quality of life (for instance their ability to hold down a job or relationship), may benefit from psychotherapy.

Managing the boundaries – where to draw the line

By taking a detailed client history at the beginning of your relationship, you can uncover potential deep-rooted issues that may require a different kind of expertise than you can provide as a life coach. Here are my suggested 'red flags' to indicate that a client *may not* be ready to work with a life coach:

- Is the client on any medication that may affect their ability to focus and concentrate? (I would simply ask for details of any medication and check myself.)
- Are they dependent on drugs (including alcohol)?
- Are they considering suicide?
- Have they been diagnosed as clinically depressed?
- Do they think they could be suffering from depression? (This may need further exploration as if there is a 'good' reason for the depression then this is unlikely to be clinical – just a normal, human reaction to a difficulty in their life.)
- Has a close family member died within the last year? (This can trigger clinical depression.)
- Have they been diagnosed with a mental health condition such a bipolar disorder?
- Is there a history of abuse – either giving or receiving it?
- Have they previously undertaken extensive counselling or psychotherapy that they consider was unsuccessful?

These questions could form part of your first session, where you can ask the client and explore further any grey areas that get mentioned. Or you could cover these points in a simple written questionnaire that clients complete and then sign to form part of an agreement. This then becomes a useful record that highlights the basic premise under which you agreed to take them on as a client. Be aware, however, that you may not always receive completely truthful answers, and you will need to be on your guard during the ongoing coaching relationship in case the client appears to be mentally unstable or unwell.

An initial meeting with a potential client before agreeing to take them on is an excellent method of checking suitability for coaching. I offer a short, no-cost telephone coaching session in the first instance, which gives an opportunity for both my client and I to decide if we are comfortable working together. Sometimes, a client's circumstances may trigger issues within you, or they have such different values to you that you realize you would find it difficult to support them. In these circumstances, I would offer my apologies and recommend another coach (or therapist or counsellor) better 'suited' to their requirements. Your 'gut reaction' when you first meet or speak with a potential new client will inform you as to whether you can work with this person. Trust your intuition if something doesn't feel right.

In addition to the above list, I have a second set of criteria to positively confirm that a client *is ready* for life coaching and likely to benefit from it:

- Can the client verbalise a goal as an outcome? (This demonstrates that the client is positive enough to think 'towards' a solution.)
- Are their goals self-referenced and self-maintained, e.g. within their control and not dependent on another person changing?
- Do they believe that they can achieve their goals? (It's okay if they see it as difficult, as long as they agree to the possibility.)
- Are they committed to honouring the coaching sessions, sticking to appointment times, and carrying out agreed actions to the best of their abilities?
- What result is the client expecting? (Ensure that expectations are realistic and provide clear information on what coaching is, and isn't.)
- Does the client have the means to fund the coaching, i.e. they are self-sufficient and have a regular income of some kind?

Once you begin to work with a client, be aware of any change in the dynamics of the relationship. Use the following questions to help you notice if your relationship is shifting towards therapy:

- How do you feel about the client?
- Do you have a strong desire to 'fix' something about the client?
- Is the client continually covering the same old ground and ceasing to make progress?
- Do you feel 'stuck' when working with the client?
- Does the client have emotional pain that they need to have relieved?
- Is the client forming an unnatural attachment to you?

- Does the client expect you to solve their problems for them?
- Is the client able to take responsibility for what happens in their life?

So, awareness and acknowledgement are paramount. Do not ignore the danger signs, rather acknowledge them and discuss with the client whether coaching is an appropriate way forward for them right now. If you do refer them, it is perfectly within reason that they will return to you at some point in the future once their current issue is resolved. And it is also possible that the client engages in both coaching and counselling at the same time, as Tatiana Bachkirova and Elaine Cox (2004: 5) explain in their excellent article 'A bridge over troubled water': 'Anyone could be engaged in both counselling and coaching processes, even at the same time if necessary and with no stigma attached.' I would add that having an open communication between yourself and the counsellor will ensure that you can each work more effectively within your separate – but sometimes overlapping – domains.

Knowing your own boundaries

Just how 'remedial' your coaching can be while still remaining effective and safe for the client will depend on your training, experience and confidence. It is extremely useful for you to explore around the 'edges' of your comfort zone so that you are clear about what kind of client you would not take on in the first place, and under what circumstances you would refer them on to a therapist or counsellor. For instance, here are some situations/clients that I have *not* taken on:

- During a first session with a client, she repeatedly blamed everyone else in her life for all the problems she was up against. However I phrased my questions to identify areas of self-directed responsibility, she would accept nothing. She was a complete 'victim' mentally, but also came across as quite forceful in her opinions, so I did not feel optimistic that life coaching would help her. I suggested that maybe she should encourage those other people in her life to come and see me, as life coaching didn't seem the appropriate route for her to take personally.

- Another woman wanted to work on building positive relationships, but it became clear quite quickly that she had some deep-rooted issues around intimacy and sexual intercourse. This I referred on to a specialist sex therapist.
- A father wanted his son to go to a life coach as he had no direction in his life and was behaving in a threatening manner – and had actually pulled a knife on his father recently. You need to consider your personal safety at all times; do not take risks.

On the other hand, here are some situations/clients that I *have* taken on, with successful outcomes:

- A man who during our first telephone conversation said he felt like 'jumping off a cliff'. I took this as a red flag and paid particular attention to his outlook and it became clear quite quickly that he was moving forwards and making progress towards his goals, and feeling very much better as a result.
- An ex-alcoholic woman who saw me about making improvements in other areas of her life, including getting fit. Alcohol seemed to be a continuing issue in her life and I was careful not to end up trying to 'treat' this directly. It did, however, crop up sometimes as an obstacle to her achieving her goals so aspects of it were discussed.

Importance of clear agreements and outcomes

For borderline clients, it is even more important to be very explicit about the nature of your relationship and the purpose of coaching. By clarifying and recording your client's goals in the first instance, you can be clear about whether what they want is remedial (looking backwards and problem focused) or self-directed and motivational (looking forwards and solution focused). Often, clients may be somewhere in the middle and the effective coach will help the client separate out their issues, understand the scope of coaching and make positive steps to achievement.

Get your client to write down and record their goals.

This is your constant central theme. It provides a fixed centrepoint around which all your questions and exercises will revolve. As long as you remain 'near' to these goals, you are unlikely to stray too far into therapeutic issues.

On the other hand, many coaching techniques teach ways of overcoming obstacles or exploring feelings or beliefs in such a way that they are clearly stepping over that boundary. For instance, many NLP techniques are designed to deal with serious mental blocks such as phobias or changing childhood beliefs. This is a necessary and often vital step in the coaching process: 'Coaches cannot avoid working with "blocks" to development with their client and for this reason, we would agree, they need to build on the body of knowledge developed in psychotherapy and counselling' (Bachkirova and Cox, 2004: 5). The key is to keep any interventions short and focused, and if they don't work, consider referring on. For example, if the obstacle becomes the key focus of ongoing sessions then the unspoken agreement you have now accepted from the client is: 'Unless you "cure" me of my obstacle I cannot achieve my goals'. This would indicate that it is time to refer the client on. Although you should not let the client's mental issues/obstacles take all your focus, equally it would be wrong to ignore or disregard them. Be prepared to ask questions about them with the intention of clarifying how close this is to the edge of coaching and how you resolve to deal with it.

How to refer on

I would suggest in the first instance that you make contact with local counsellors and therapists and find out more about what they do and the specialisms that they have. In this way you create a bank of appropriate experts to whom you can refer people. They may also pass clients your way, as after someone has completed counselling or psychotherapy it may be an ideal time to take up the services of a life coach.

The clearer you can present what you offer to potential clients, the easier it becomes to explain when you feel your service doesn't match their requirements. Having an initial session offered as an opportunity for you both to decide whether to work together, gives you an appropriate time to say that at this time, based on what they have explained to you about the nature of their problems, you feel it would be more beneficial for them to see a counsellor/psychotherapist, and offer to give them details of those you would recommend. If they insist that they want life coaching, I would take this to be a further red flag and personally I would not concede.

If it becomes a growing concern with an existing client, it may be harder to break the relationship. If you feel it appropriate then you need to explain to the client why you feel this and point out that it may not be in their best interests to continue coaching. Always let the client know you would be happy to work with them again once the issue is resolved.

Adhering to a code of ethics

By belonging to a professional coaching association, such as the Association for Coaching, as a member you will be asked to abide by their own code of ethics and good practice. This will help provide you with a working framework to guide and support you in making decisions about the kind of work you do and who you do it for, in relation to any boundary issues (Association for Coaching, 2008b).

The importance of supervision

Occasionally as a coach you will experience client situations that stretch you, leave you feeling uncomfortable or somehow 'hook' you into their patterns of behaviour. In order to deal with these situations effectively and enable you to let them go, you need to work with a trained coach supervisor/mentor with whom you can share the details of the coach–client relationship.

One key benefit that can be gained from regular, in-depth supervision is having someone outside of the coach–client relationship explore those boundaries and help you recognize potential dangers. Supervision is a safe and supportive environment for a coach to explore the bridge between coaching and therapy and make ethical decisions on appropriate ways to deal with clients. Supervision will be explored in more depth in the next chapter.

Summary

- Understanding the difference between coaching and therapy is important for the protection of both your client and yourself.
- The crucial difference is in the intent of a coach – to focus on the client's goal and how to move forwards towards it.
- You need to confirm as best you can that a client is 'fit' for coaching by asking key questions at the outset of your relationship – and being on your guard during the whole relationship.
- The boundary between coaching and therapy is not a clear line, and will be different for every practitioner. You must decide on your own criteria.
- Setting clear outcomes at the start of the relationship sets client expectations and protects you.
- Be willing to refer clients on for therapy if you feel it more appropriate.
- As a member of a professional body, follow their code of ethics, which will provide you with guidance on where to draw the line.
- Supervision is a safe environment for you to explore potential boundary issues and highlight whether you are being 'hooked' by a client's mental patterns.

14

Developing your skills

With such a vast array of competencies to develop and skills to gain, where does the fledgling coach begin to develop and enhance these skills? And as for the more experienced, how do they ensure that their skills remain sharp? This book has provided you with many exercises and examples to think about and use, however it is unlikely to satisfy all your developmental needs.

Undertake specific coach training

Depending on the skills you may have already acquired from training and/or experience in an associated profession, you may choose to undertake specific coach training ranging from an extensive long-term programme of development (such as the Oxford Brookes University's Certificate, Diploma and MA in coaching and mentoring) to short specialist techniques (such as clean language training offered by many organizations including my own: www.cleancoaching.com) to a wealth of short- to medium-term coach training programmes in between.

Before you begin searching for appropriate coach training, be clear on the specific reasons that you have for undertaking training, as this will impact on your choice. In addition to developing your skills, you may want the training to give you credibility and respect in the market through having a recognized and respected qualification. In which case, you will need to take into account the reputation and public recognition of the coach training organization in question.

You may want training to build your confidence as a coach, in which case go for a training course that incorporates lots of practice and feedback, not just theoretical models and written assignments. You may want training to incorporate all aspects of running a coach business, not just the specific skills of a coach, but also managing a client session, contracting, legal responsibilities, marketing your practice, etc. Again, take your time to ensure that the syllabus contains all that you require.

Some coach training programmes are two days long. Some are three years plus. Some provide distance learning by the internet and/or by telephone. Be realistic about what you can expect to learn given the duration and delivery mechanism, also based on your current skills level. Do you need a 'top-up' or a complete overhaul?

You can investigate available coach training programmes through the main professional coaching bodies' websites. The Association for Coaching lists recognized training programmes, and the International Coaching Federation has accredited coach training programmes. For a good resource that shows a very wide range of different programmes, see Coaching and Mentoring Network (© Coaching and Mentoring Network Ltd, 2008).

I cannot recommend specific coach training programmes, but what I can recommend is that you research thoroughly and prepare specific questions to ask each training provider, some examples of which are given below:

- For how long has this course been running?
- How many coaches have completed it and qualified?
- Have any failed and how do you manage that situation?
- How do you assess the quality of the training you deliver?
- What evidence can you provide of that quality?
- What standard do you expect a coach to have achieved before they undertake your course?
- What standard do you expect a coach to have achieved having completed your course?
- How do you assess if they have reached that standard?
- What would you see as the next development step for a coach, having completed your course?

- What is the specific content of the course (i.e. the syllabus)?
- What range of training methods are used? (Consider whether they suit your learning style, i.e. the mix of practical, theoretical, reflective and experimental.)
- What information do you have on the ongoing success of previously trained coaches?
- How many have gone on to become successful full-time coaches?
- Can you provide contact details of a successful coach who has completed the course?
- Who are the tutors for this course and what is their background?
- Can I talk/meet with them before deciding to enrol?
- There are many different coach training courses available. What makes yours special and unique and why should I choose it?

Having explored all these questions with the various coach training organizations that you are interested in, you also need to take the following into consideration before making your final decision:

- *timing* – is the training available at the times and dates that you require?
- *cost* – can you afford it and do you feel it represents good value for money?
- *motivation* – do you feel excited and enthusiastic about the training having learnt more about it?
- *values* – how well do the course tutors/syllabus seem aligned to your own values as a coach?

Supervision

Supervision is a hot topic in the UK coach community at the moment, with a cross-section of differing opinions on what supervision is, whether coaches require it and how it should be regulated. I personally see incredible value in having a supervisor. This person enables me to explore my coach–client relationships and identify my own potential blind spots, sore spots, projections or distortions. This means that supervision makes me a better coach, as well as helping me realize any of my own personal issues that might still need further exploration and resolution. Also, this makes my life coaching business more attractive to potential clients, as I can explain how supervision gives the client some quality assurance too.

For corporate coaches, supervision is becoming a standard requirement that businesses will look for and expect evidence of when choosing a coach. All the coaching professional bodies expect accredited members to commit to some kind of regular supervision, although they don't yet specify appropriate supervisor training or qualifications.

What is supervision?

If we break the word into its two component parts we get a good sense of what the process of supervision entails. 'Super' vision means that an independent person is taking a wider view of your coaching. That 'vision' is as impartial as possible, and taken from a variety of different perspectives. The wider perspective is then fed back to you to expand your awareness of what is happening for you as a coach during client sessions.

The supervisor is not expected to be present in the client session, however the coach brings with them details of the client to the supervision session and explain the 'story so far'. The supervisor listens and asks questions, as a coach would. But rather than aim for a specific goal, the supervisor's role is to provide knowledge and insight from taking that wider perspective. What the coach does with the information they get is up to them. The supervisor has no 'power' over a coach as a work supervisor would have. They can encourage and advise however, and help a coach improve their skills through greater self-awareness.

How is supervision conducted?

This is a brand new field, and as with coaches, supervisors are emerging from different backgrounds and professions and conducting supervision in a different fashion depending on this. Some see supervision as super-coaching, i.e. coaching for a coach, so all the same models and processes would be used. Some come from a therapeutic or psychological background, where there are clear guidelines on how supervision should be conducted for clinical practitioners.

As with coaching, we will see clearer definitions and examples of best practice develop over the next few years. One model used for supervision is the seven-eyed model of supervision, developed by Peter Hawkins and Robin Shohet (1989). This gives a framework of seven different perspectives that a supervisor can use to help a coach view their relationship with a client. In summary, these are:

1 the coachee's system;
2 the coach's interventions;
3 the relationship between the coach and the client;
4 the coach themselves;
5 the 'parallel process', how the coach may be inadvertently mirroring the client's system with the supervisor here and now;
6 the supervisor's self-reflection; what is happening for them right now?
7 the wider context, including all other possible perspectives, ethical, legal, etc.

The mechanics of supervision

How often should you see a supervisor and long should a supervision session last? Does it need to be conducted in person or would a telephone session suffice? How about email updates and feedback? Different opinions exist and you need to consider what will suit you best, given your location and the number of active clients you are working with. There is no point in having a weekly session of supervision lasting an hour when you only have two active clients. So, arrange your supervision sessions in line with the volume of actual coaching you are actively involved in. A reasonable ratio to guide the amount of supervision you undertake would be around one hour of supervision for every 15–20 hours of coaching.

You can have one-to-one supervision sessions, or alternatively many supervisors offer sessions in small groups. As an inexperienced coach, the more experience your supervisor has of coaching the better. As a more experienced coach, you may decide to arrange peer supervision, working in tandem with another experienced coach and providing supervision for each other. Both peer supervision and group coaching offer a cost-effective solution to regular supervision.

Finding a suitable supervisor

Finding the right supervisor could be a challenge as there are currently so few that are fully trained and advertise their services. Your first port of call is any coaching professional body that you belong to. They can offer you advice about how to choose a supervisor and may have lists of known supervisors who adhere to certain codes of ethics.

As with training, draw up a list of potential supervisors who offer the right kind of service in the right kind of format, and speak to each of them to gain more detail. As well as their background, experience and appropriate qualifications, consider their skills. A good supervisor will be a fantastic coach in their own right. Most importantly, you need to feel comfortable with the person and sense that you have a good match in terms of personality, style, ethics and values. Having a 'trial' supervisory session would be preferable, before making a long-term, ongoing commitment.

Becoming an accredited coach

For many, this is a natural progression for the experienced professional coach to make when they have enough evidence to support their application. At the moment in the UK, you can apply for accreditation with the Association for Coaching and the International Coach Federation. The Association for Coaching process requires a minimum of five years' experience as a coach and 250 hours of coaching activity. The International Coach Federation has a range of accreditation levels with different criteria, and a written and oral examination is also necessary.

Accreditation is already looked for and valued by organizations purchasing coaching and as the life coaching market matures, many individual life coach customers will also seek this as a legitimate stamp of approval of a coach's experience.

Co-coaching

Co-coaching is the practice of coaching among coaches, the purpose of which is to develop and enhance one's coaching ability by observing others and receiving feedback on one's own coaching. It provides an opportunity to reflect on your coaching style, and to experience and experiment with new coaching techniques. Many groups exist around the UK for the sole purpose of practising co-coaching in this fashion. The Association for Coaching has regional co-coaching forums across the country and a large and growing number of active participants.

Co-coaching is a three-way learning opportunity:

- being coached by others;
- observing others being coached;
- coaching others on their coaching technique.

You can discover an amazing range of coaching methods and styles that have developed to satisfy different needs and circumstances, and so benchmark your own practice. Effective co-coaching forums are run by experienced coaches and facilitators following best practice guidelines. These ensure that maximum time is spent actually practising coaching rather than just discussing it, and that new ideas and fresh techniques are continually investigated and explored.

The benefits of co-coaching

A local co-coaching group is likely to be set up on a non-profit basis, so attendance is either free or very low cost to cover financial outlays. So, it provides a great learning opportunity for a low investment. Attendance at a co-coaching forum should be counted as part of your continuous professional development (CPD) (see later in this chapter) so you can use this if you are going for accreditation. Life coaching can be a lonely business at times, and regular attendance at a local co-coaching group provides you with a network of like-minded people, with whom you can relate and share success stories, ideas and resources.

Techniques for the practice of co-coaching

There are many ways to facilitate a co-coaching practice session, which are continually being developed through experimentation. Current methods I know of include different group structures such as small groups, triads, quads or large group activities. Also, different processes are tried out, which may include structured exercises where coach and client have certain guidelines to the session, e.g. a short time limit, sharing alternative questions with a second coach, or the client is silent (does not answer the question but simply internalizes it and then comments on its effect), etc. What is important is that role of the observer or 'meta coach' is fully utilized and adequate time is spent on the observer giving feedback on the coaching session, and using all their coaching skills in the effective delivery of that feedback.

Learning from your own mistakes

Spending time on self-reflection following each and every client coaching session, enables you to be aware of your own developing coach habits, to recognize possible danger areas and take steps to improve on this before it results in reduced quality for the client. From my own personal experience and what other coaches have shared with me, the following are some possible mistakes that are commonly made by the newly trained coach:

Becoming more attached to the results than the client

In the early days of my coaching practice, I believe I made this mistake on more than one occasion. Although I had a good understanding of coaching and adequate training, I still had a belief that somehow I was going to solve people's problems for them, be a catalyst for change and help people to achieve things. All admirable beliefs at first glance, however the responsibility to bring about change was with me, not the client.

As my coaching practice was aimed at single people looking to establish new friendships and potentially start a new relationship, I quickly realized that I judged myself very harshly if, after the package of 90 days' coaching, there was no significant movement towards a relationship. Now I can see how wrong that was. All my clients were delighted with the impact of the coaching, most of them saw it as a process of self-discovery and measured the success of coaching in terms of shifts in attitude rather than tangible changes in circumstances.

The more I have been involved with coaching, the more I have understood the importance of client ownership. This is a common problem for new coaches. If you ask any coach why they chose life coaching as a profession, they are likely to say something about needing to help others. Could it be that anyone who actually *wants* to coach is probably in danger of getting too attached to the result? The mistake then manifested itself in my attitude towards the coaching session. I invested a great deal of personal energy, which actually resulted in me feeling burnt-out in under a year. I think some of my coaching behaviours were also undermined by my blinkered focus on the end result. For instance, I might have felt impatient and not listened as well if the client were talking of an incidental point, or something that happened in the past. I may have rushed the client a little with the direction and delivery of my questions, and may not have paused for long enough between questions. Towards the end of a session I would feel even more compelled to bring things to an action-oriented conclusion, so I may have sounded rushed, or sometimes over-ran a session to ensure that things were 'completed' to my satisfaction.

Why did this mistake happen? It was probably due to my inexperience. I didn't yet have that deep conviction that the only person who can solve the client's problem is the client themselves. The practical actions I took to resolve the problem were first to have further coach training in clean language. The philosophy behind the questioning technique is geared to ensuring that the coach keeps their own issues out of the way of the client. By practising clean language questions I learnt how to stop influencing the client with my own agenda.

This new understanding changed the way I explained my coaching services to potential clients. I made it clear to people that they will be doing the work to change themselves during the coaching process, not me. And I also added to my coaching agreement that the client must take 100 per cent responsibility for their goals and actions.

Not quantifying the intensity of how the client feels about something

I never used to ask questions around 'On a scale of 1 to 10, how much do you feel. . .'. This meant that sometimes I thought that a particular feeling or emotion a client might have either was much more significant than the reality, or sometimes I could seriously underestimate its importance. This was a particular issue over the telephone, when I didn't have visual sensory acuity to help me, just vocal change clues and cues.

A tangible negative that occurred with a couple of clients was when I asked for their commitment to carry out certain actions before the next session: they gave it, but didn't follow through. Had I ask how motivated they were on a scale of 1 to 10 to carry out their actions, I think I would have discovered that it was very low. This could have given me the opportunity to ask 'What needs to happen for you to increase your motivation from (say) a 5 to a 10?'. Why did this mistake happen? I had never covered this aspect of coaching much in any of my training. When I learnt about it I thought it would be a good idea. Once I started to use it regularly I could see how essential it was. It is useful if you check not only commitment levels, but also the intensity and importance of other factors, such as emotions, values or positive states of mind.

Getting 'hooked' into the client's pattern of behaviour

This is when you suddenly realize that the client has been bemoaning how much of a bully his wife is, and you find yourself inexplicably caught up in frustration and want to order this man to stand up for himself. To understand how easily this kind of mistake can happen is to be aware of how relationships act as systems and one person's habitual behaviours and responses are likely to 'hook' you into the roles that they already have around them in their lives. Good supervision will help you to recognize if this is in danger of happening with any of your clients. Also, be aware of any inappropriate strong feelings or emotions that come up for you during the client session. Be sure to discuss this with your supervisor.

Running out of steam

If you have a standard repertoire of techniques, processes and exercises that you use with clients, there is a danger that after a certain number of sessions you will find yourself running out of steam. 'What can I try next on them?', you are thinking. Ideally, you will not develop a predictable 'curriculum' of activities, but treat each client as an individual and take a fresh look at what might be appropriate each and every time you work with them.

Getting too comfortable with your favourite approaches

As above, you may find that after a while you are drifting towards a 'standard' set of processes and techniques. This may indicate that it's time for you to seek some fresh training in order to develop some new approaches. Certainly, attendance at a co-coaching group will help you explore alternative approaches and may spark some ideas for further training activities and areas.

Continuous professional development

CPD is a formalized process for maintaining and enhancing the skills and knowledge, as well as developing the personal qualities appropriate for your profession. It is considered to be an ongoing and continuous activity, as learning and development is seen as a lifelong activity of improvement, rather than ever reaching a specific level of perfect competence.

All professional coaching associations will provide you with CPD guidance, and you may want to formalize your CPD in order to apply for coaching accreditation. You will need to keep records, usually in the form of CPD certificates issued as part of CPD activities and events, and your own CPD log of activities. Your log will highlight the development goals you set for yourself (typically over a 12-month period), what activities you undertook and when, the duration of each activity and finally what you learned from each.

Although CPD is a formal process, the actual elements that make up your CPD will be selected by you and will be unique to you, depending on your personal goals for developing as a professional coach. As well as the obvious workshops, events and short courses, other activities on your CPD log could include:

- *inputs*, such as:
  - Distance learning;
  - Reading relevant books;
  - Subscription to a professional journal;
- *outputs*, such as:
  - speaking at a conference;
  - writing an article.

The key benefits to CPD is that the process encourages you to plan for appropriate ongoing learning and development and provides a framework within which both formal and informal learning activities can be set. The ultimate goal is to improve personal performance and career/business progression.

Developing coaching skills – a lifelong journey

One of the most wonderful things about the profession of coaching is that it is such an expansive field, which has many streams of knowledge flowing into it. Over time, more and more rivers of coaching specialisms will emerge and I am convinced that we will see growth in the quantity and the quality of UK coaches.

In writing this book it was difficult to find a place to stop, as each topic led to further research and more doors of opportunity opened in turn. I look forward to the future of coaching and hope that this book has served as a map to help you navigate your own coaching skills journey.

Summary

- Consider coach training that is appropriate to your requirements, and thoroughly investigate the options that exist.
- Consider coach supervision options and recognize the value of having a super-view and wider perspective to enable you to grow your ability and your practice.
- Coach accreditation presents an opportunity for you to gain a seal of approval on your ability and experience as a coach.
- Co-coaching is an excellent high-value but low-cost method to refresh your skills, learn new ones and receive peer feedback on your actual coaching skills and techniques.
- Continuous professional development is likely to be a necessity for accreditation, but also a valuable process for you to plan your ongoing development and recognize that all learning is a constant and continuous journey of discovery.

Notes

1 The ICF survey involved contacting 30,000 known coaches with apparently valid email addresses. 'Whilst the figure of 50,000 coaches worldwide has often been quoted, a more prudent approach . . . would be to take the 30,000 figure as at least a base line' (International Coach Federation, 2008, p 15).
2 Access to the Toluna poll can be gained through the following link: http://uk.toluna.com/polls/42006/ Excluding_Sports_coaching,_which_of_the_following_best_ describes_you? (accessed 28 June 2008).

References

Association for Coaching (2004) *Summary Report: UK Coaching Rates*, Online, Available at www.associationforcoaching.com/memb/UKcrs104.pdf (accessed 28 June 2008).

Association for Coaching (2005) *AC Competency Framework*, Online, Available at www.associationforcoaching.com/about/ACCFrame.pdf (accessed 30 July 2008).

Association for Coaching (2008a) *Coaching Definitions*, Online, Available at www.associationforcoaching.com/about/about03.htm (accessed 28 June 2008).

Association for Coaching (2008b) *Code of Ethics and Good Practice*, Online, Available at www.associationforcoaching.com/about/about02.htm (accessed 5 July 2008).

Association for Coaching (2008c) *Statement of Shared Professional Values*, Online, Available at www.associationforcoaching.com/news/M80221.htm (accessed 17 July 2008).

Bachkirova, T. and Cox, E. (2004) A bridge over troubled water, *Counselling at Work*, Spring 2005: 2–9 © *European Mentoring and Coaching*, 11 (1).

BACP (British Association for Counselling and Psychotherapy) (nd) *What is Counselling?*, Online, Available at www.bacp.co.uk/information/education/whatiscounselling.php (accessed 5 July 2008).

Bandler, R. and Grinder, J. (1976) *The Structure of Magic*, California, CA: Science and Behavior Books.

Barber, J. (2005) *Good Question! The Art of Asking Questions to Bring About Positive Change*, La Murta, Spain: Lean Marketing Press.

Bateson, G. (2000) *Steps to an Ecology of Mind: Collected Essays in Anthropology, Psychiatry, Evolution and Epistemology* (new edition), Chicago, IL: Chicago University Press.

Berne, E. (1967) *Games People Play*, New York: Grove Press.

Bodenhamer, B. and Hall, L. (2002) *The User's Manual for the Brain*, Carmarthen: Crown House Publishing.

Coaching and Mentoring Network Ltd (2008) *Training and Accreditation*, Online, Authors Anna Britnor Guest and Pauline Willis (unless otherwise stated), Available at www.coachingnetwork.org.uk/ResourceCentre/TrainingAndAccreditation (accessed 15 July 2008).

Dilts, R. (1990) *Changing Belief Systems with Neuro-Linguistic Programming*, Capitola, CA: Meta Publications.

Gallwey, T. (1974) *The Inner Game of Tennis*, New York: Random House.

Gladwell, M. (2005) *Blink: The Power of Thinking Without Thinking*, Boston, MA: Little, Brown and Company.

Grant, A. (2003) 'The impact on life coaching on goal attainment, metacognition and mental health', *Social Behaviour and Personality*, 31(3): 253–264.

Grant, A. (2006) 'Solution-focused coaching', in J. Passmore (ed) *Excellence in Coaching: The Industry Guide*, London: Kogan Page.

Grodzki, L. and Allen, W. (2005) *The Business and Practice of Coaching: Finding Your Niche, Making Money, and Attracting Ideal Clients*, New York: W. W. Norton.

Hawkins, P. and Shohet, R. (1989) *Supervision in the Helping Profession*, Milton Keynes: Open University Press.

Hermanns, W. (1983) *Einstein and the Poet: In Search of the Cosmic Man*, Brookline Village, MA: Branden Books.

Hodgkinson, G. P., Langan-Fox, J. and Sadler-Smith, E. (2008) 'Intuition: a fundamental bridging construct in the behavioural sciences', *British Journal of Psychology*, 99: 1–27.

International Coach Federation (2008) *ICF Code of Ethics*, PricewaterhouseCoopers, London. Online, Available at www.coachfederation.org/about-icf/ethics-&-regulation/icf-code-of-ethics/ (accessed 5 April 2009).

Jung, C. (1964) *Man and his Symbols*, London: Aldus Books Ltd.

Jung, C. (1992) *Psychological Types (Collected Works of C.G. Jung)* (revised edition), Princeton, NJ: Princeton University Press.

Kipling, R. (1902) *The Elephant's Child*, Available online at http://www.online-literature.com/kipling/165/

Kline, N. (1999) *Time to Think*, London: Ward Lock.

Knaster, M. (1996) *Discovering the Body's Wisdom*, New York: Bantam Books.

Lakoff, G. and Johnson, M. (1980) *Metaphors We Live By*, Chicago, IL: University of Chicago Press.

McDermott, I. and Jago, W. (2001) *The NLP Coach*, London: Judy Piatkus (Publishers).

McNamara, H. (2007) *Niche Marketing for Coaches*, London: Thorogood.

Martin, C. (2001) *The Life Coaching Handbook*, Carmarthen: Crown House Publishing.

Miller, W. and Rollnick, S. (2002) *Motivational Interviewing: Preparing people for change* (2nd edition), New York: Guilford Press.

Perkins, D. (2002) *Meaning of Intuition,* Online, Available at www.gse.harvard.edu/~t656_web/My_contributions/Meaning_of_intuition.htm (accessed 1 July 2008).

Peter L.J. (1977) *Peter's Quotations: Ideas for Our Time,* New York: William Morrow & Co.

Pinker, S. (1997) *How the Mind Works,* New York: W. W. Norton.

Prochaska, J. and DiClemente, C. (1983) 'Stages and processes of self-change of smoking: toward an integrative model of change', *Journal of Consulting and Clinical Psychology,* 51(3): 390–395.

Rogers, J. (2004) *Coaching Skills: A Handbook,* Milton Keynes: Open University Press.

Starr, J. (2008) *The Coaching Manual* (2nd edition), Harlow: Pearson Education.

Tompkins, P. and Lawley, J. (2000) *Metaphors in Mind: Transformation through Symbolic Modelling,* London: The Developing Company Press.

UK Council for Psychotherapy (2008) *Frequently Asked Questions,* Online, Available at www.psychotherapy.org.uk/iqs/sid.00527940458747857603036/faqs.html (accessed 5 July 2008).

Whitmore, J. (2002) *Coaching for Performance* (3rd edition), London: Nicholas Brealey.

Whitworth, L., Kimsey-House, K., Kimsey-House, H. and Sandahl, P. (2007) *Co-Active Coaching: New Skills for Coaching People Towards Success in Work and Life* (2nd edition), Mountain View, CA: Davies-Black Publishing.

Wilson, C. (2007) *Best Practice in Performance Coaching,* London: Kogan Page.

Index